POPULATION ETHICS

Population Ethics

EDITED BY
FRANCIS X. QUINN

CORPUS BOOKS
Washington—Cleveland

Corpus Instrumentorum, Inc.
1330 Massachusetts Ave., N.W.
Washington, D.C. 20005

First Printing 1968

Library of Congress Catalog Card Number: 68–10452

PRINTED IN THE UNITED STATES OF AMERICA

Contents

FRANCIS X. QUINN

Introduction

Every second on the clock one more person is born. At
that prevailing rate, the population of the United States
increases each year by some three million. Located in
the lobby of the Department of Commerce building in
Washington, D.C., is a large chart that shows the estimated size of the population of the United States. In
the spring of 1960, the estimate reached 180 million, a
number indicating that more than thirty million people
had been added in the 1950's. As we begin our discussion
of the problems of population, the population clock reads
200 million, and is still climbing. While the population
of the U.S. increases by three million annually, the
population of India increases by eight million, that of
China by fifteen and the world as a whole by forty-five
million. The growth of human population has been
compared to the human pulse rate. Every time your pulse
throbs, assuming that you have a normal pulse beat, the
population of the world will have been increased by more
than one human being.

Exact population statistics pose many problems. There is no way of registering the daily births and deaths for much of Asia, Africa, and South America. But the experts are in close agreement about the figures: somewhere between 80 and 100 individuals are added every minute to the total world population. On the average, about 270,000 babies are born every day, and about 142,000 people die—resulting in a gain of about 128,000. This adds up to a total approximating forty-eight million additional humans every year.

This yearly increase raises many different questions. Can per-capita food output supply the growing population? How does population growth affect developing areas? How does it affect the American economy? Do the facts and consequent problems of population growth necessitate a re-examination of our population policy? How does the problem of population control affect the Catholic family? In view of scientific advances and the complexity of population problems, what and why is the Catholic Church teaching about conjugal morality? The following essays provide a perspective on these questions. We have selected five outstanding scholars to view each of these questions on the population problem and invited them to speak for themselves.

Dr. Lester Brown, Staff Economist for the U.S. Department of Agriculture, addresses himself to the problem of population growth in relation to the food supply. Students of resource problems tend to divide rather sharply into optimists and pessimists. So far the human species has been undeniably successful—whether success is measured by sheer numbers or by the power of reshaping nature for human purposes. This success has resulted in great measure from the development of science and technology, and the optimists place their faith in man's ability to continue this development indefinitely. The pessimists insist that we have no evidence that man's ingenuity is thus unlimited. Certainly, man is often wasteful and destructive; devastated landscapes, polluted waters, and decaying cities are cited as examples that progress is not automatically continuous. The pessimists focus on the immense problems of the underdeveloped regions; the optimists are apt to be mostly concerned with the Western world and the challenge of space. Dr. Brown describes the food-population problem that is geographically confined to the less developed regions. But he reminds us that we of the developed nations are equally committed to its solution.

Dr. Irene B. Taeuber, Senior Research Demographer for the Office of Population Research at Princeton University, discusses the change and the future of the population of the developing areas. There is wide disparity among the peoples of the world in per-capita income, in health, in education. Differences in wealth among nations have always existed, but in our space age, rapid communication and transportation have converted the earth into a neighborhood where great differences in prosperity and comfort are less and less tolerable. Improvements in diet and health are a beginning, but capital and technical know-how are needed for a modern economy. The problem is further complicated by the fact that the poorest nations are multiplying at the fastest rates.

The land surface of the earth covers approximately fifty-eight million square miles, so that if people were distributed evenly, there would be about fifty per square mile. The distribution is far from even: almost half of the land surface is presently unsuitable for human settlement because of unfavorable climate or soil. Two-thirds of the 3.3 billion total population live crowded into about 4.2 million square miles—7.3 per cent of the total land surface. These densely populated areas include much of the Far East, India, parts of the East Indies, Western and Central Europe, and the northeastern United States. The rapid rate of population increase is related not so much to density as to the degree of economic development. The highly industrialized nations are not growing so fast as those with economies based primarily on agriculture. Further, the higher the educational level, the slower the growth rate. These facts pose all sorts of problems in relation to economic and educational development. Dr. Taeuber summarizes the results emerging from studies of developing areas and assures us that the roles and the responsibilities of the demographers and behavioral scientists will not be antiquated in the near future.

Dr. Alice M. Rivlin, Deputy Assistant Secretary for Program Analysis, Department of Health, Education and Welfare, analyzes the effect of population growth on American economy. The U.S. constitution stated that an enumeration of the population "be made within three years after the first meeting of the Congress of the United States and within every subsequent term of ten years." The first census was made in 1790, reporting a population of 3,329,214. The count has been repeated each tenth year ever since, to the 1960 census that reported a total of 179,323,175. The history of population growth in the United States can thus be followed in some detail for a period of 170 years. We have absorbed an expanding population with continuing increases in per-capita output. Can we continue to do so?

Father John L. Thomas, S.J., of the Cambridge Center for Social Studies, calls for a clear and thorough reinterpretation of the personal and social significance of human sexuality, as well as for a thoughtful restructuring of the relationships relevant to the development, expression, and regulation of sexuality. There is need to develop and to explain a philosophy of human sexuality that will take into consideration modern man's changed relationship to reproduction and that will give due weight to the procreational aspects of marital relations. Father Thomas, an expert on the Catholic family, then studies how the traditional attitudes and practices relating to sex, marriage, and family are affected by our rapid transition to an industrialized urban society. Any negative attitude toward sex leaves couples poorly prepared to integrate sex, love, and self-control in marriage. The continued observance of Christian marriage ideals appears likely only if Catholic couples acquire a more adequate understanding and appreciation of the Church's positive doctrine concerning the vocation of marriage, together with the firm conviction that this doctrine remains currently relevant.

Father George Wilson, S.J., Professor of Sacramental Theology at Woodstock College, Woodstock, Md., explains the Church's positive doctrine on conjugal morality, and explores the Church's position toward contraception.

The reason for this volume is evident. We have never before had to face the problem of world population with all its human, social, ethical, and moral implications. Many people are trying to influence public opinion on the subject. Exaggerated expression of views has led to controversy and misunderstanding. But simple facts, explanatory theories, and predictions make little sense unless they are related to the question of human values and ethics. If we are to act responsibly, we must reflect on the problems and the goals of international society, the family, and the individual.

No one volume on such a difficult problem could hope to provide a panacea. Much significant material has already been written about this problem; but who will deny that there is much yet to be said and to be reflected upon? It is our hope that these pages may shed some new light on the magnitude of this area of concern, and that they may facilitate some of that insight and understanding necessary for arriving at a solution.

I extend my gratitude to Rev. Joseph M. Hamernick, S.J., of the University of Scranton, for his cooperation, and to Mrs. Frances Nilsson, who helped to prepare the manuscript.

LESTER R. BROWN

Population Growth and Per-Capita Food Output

The food problem is likely to be one of the most important, perhaps *the* most important problem we will face between now and the end of the century. Much of the literature dealing with this problem is devoted to answering the wrong questions. It is difficult enough to get the right answers when the right questions are asked, but it is almost impossible to get the right answers when the wrong questions are posed. For example, one of the questions frequently asked is: "How much land can be brought under cultivation?" But this is not really the relevant question; the relevant question is: "At what cost can additional land be brought under cultivation?" Someone must pay the cost of land reclamation; given enough capital to invest, there are very few areas that cannot be made to produce food.

Another question often asked and discussed at length is: "How many people can the earth support?" But this is only part of the question. The other part, and an equally relevant part, is: "At what level?" Are they to be supported at subsistence level, that is, with just enough food to maintain life? Or are they to be well-nourished so that they may lead full, active lives?

The third and related question frequently posed is: "What is the potential for expanding food output?" This is an interesting and useful question, but the really relevant one is: "What are the prospects for expanding food output?" With food shortages growing larger with each passing year, we can no longer content ourselves with simply discussing potential. We must discuss whether or not this potential can be realized as rapidly as current rates of population growth require.

Many other persistent sources of confusion associated with the food problem persist. Weather always seems to get the blame for any food shortages. It covers up a multitude of shortcomings, bureaucratic and otherwise. If there is a poor crop in India, bad weather always gets the blame. In the fall of 1963, the Soviet Union suffered a very large grain deficit, and shifted abruptly from an export position in 1962 to an import position in late 1963. It became the world's largest wheat importer in the course of a year—and the weather was responsible. At least it was deemed responsible in September and October; but by January there was talk of reorganizing the farm system and building fertilizer plants.

The difficulty of solving the food problem is often underestimated because of the tendency to project food production by extrapolating postwar production trends, say from 1950 to 1960. But in fact much of the progress made in increasing food output, either in terms of yield per acre or output per person, from 1950 to 1960 or from the end of World War II to 1960, was largely recovery from the disruption and destruction caused by the war.

Per-capita food output in the less developed regions dipped sharply during World War II, largely as a result of loss of fertilizer supplies and the destruction of irrigation systems. During the postwar period, output began to trend upward. Much progress was made during the Fifties and things appeared to be going well. But then in the early Sixties, per-capita output began to decline in both Latin America and in Asia. Food output per person in Latin America has dropped some six per cent from the postwar high reached in 1958. Food output per person in mainland China, also reaching a postwar high in 1958, has dropped even more than in Latin America. In Asia, excluding mainland China, the postwar high was reached in 1961 and has declined three or four per cent in the years since.

One of the biggest obstacles to solving the food problem is the idea that the problem itself is something far in the future—something that can be put off indefinitely. In terms of malnutrition, undernutrition, or plain hunger, however, the food problem is very much with us now, and it is likely to become worse in the less developed regions before it becomes better.

What in fact is the nutritional status of diets in the less developed regions? Some three years ago, the Department of Agriculture undertook a study to determine the nutritional adequacy of diets in some eighty major countries. Five basic nutritional indicators were chosen. The criteria were calorie intake per person, animal protein consumption, pulse protein consumption, total

protein intake, and fat intake. Minimal consumption
standards were determined by the nutritionists of both
the Food and Agricultural Organization of the United
Nations and the Department of Agriculture. They varied
according to geographic regions, climate, and average
body size. These minimal consumption levels were then
compared with actual consumption levels in these
countries. There were no diet deficits in the developed
regions. The average diet per person in the countries
in North America, Western Europe, Eastern Europe, and
Oceania (Australia and New Zealand) were adequate by
every one of the five nutritional indicators. But in the
less developed regions—Asia, Africa, and Latin America—
nutritional deficits were widespread. Thirty-six countries
containing more than half of the world's people suffered
from food energy shortages. They were not getting
enough calories to maintain normal everyday activity.
In ten countries there were serious shortages of animal
protein. These ten countries included all the bigger
countries: India, China, and Pakistan. And they also
contain almost half the world's people.

Standards used were indeed minimal, because in the
case of animal protein, for instance, the intake per person
per day was set at seven grams. Any countries in which
average intake was above seven grams were considered
to have an adequate diet, and those below, inadequate.
The standard of seven grams per person per day compares
with an average daily intake in this country of sixty-six
grams per person per day. The reference standard used
for this basic nutritional indicator was about one-tenth
of our current consumption level.

Deficits in pulse protein were relatively minor. Only

ten countries, for the most part small ones, had pulse protein deficits. In the case of total protein, deficits were widespread. Countries containing fifty-five per cent of the world's people had average diets deficit in protein. Fat deficits, though common, were not so widespread as protein deficits.

Having considered these factors of the world's food problem from a nutritional point of view, let us now look at the pattern of world food trade over the last quarter of a century in terms of economic regions. The world divides readily into developed and less developed regions. The less developed world includes Asia, Africa, and Latin America; the developed world includes the remaining regions. Before World War II there was a net flow of grain from the less developed world to the developed world averaging eleven million tons per year. During the World War II period, this flow was reversed. From 1948 to 1952, food moved from the developed world to the less developed world at the rate of four million tons of grain per year. In the years 1957 to 1959 this had become thirteen million tons; by 1960 it was twenty million tons; and preliminary estimates for 1964 showed twenty-five million tons.

Given these observations on nutritional status and on the pattern of food trade, one thing is quite clear: the less developed world is losing the capacity to feed itself. Stated otherwise: a growing share of each year's population increment is being sustained by food shipments from the developed world, largely from the United States under the Food for Peace Program.

There are some very basic differences between the conditions under which the now advanced industrial countries developed and those under which the less developed countries are now attempting to develop. What are the differences in the population-land relationship between the first countries to industrialize and those which are attempting to develop now?

The differences are many, most of them unfavorable to the countries now attempting to develop. In the first place, the area of agricultural land per person is only a fraction of what it was in the group of countries that developed earlier. Second, population growth rates are far higher, in most cases at least twice as high. Third, many of the countries which are now trying to develop have used up all the new land which can readily be brought under cultivation before developing a modern, highly pro- ductive agriculture. Fourth, the area of cultivable land per person is declining far more rapidly. And finally, significant opportunities for large scale emigration no longer exist; there is no New World to be settled; no great frontiers remain.

We noted earlier that the less developed world is losing the capacity to feed itself. Why is this? The answer can be stated simply. Historically, food output was expanded by increasing the area under cultivation, but now opportunities for such expansion are quite limited in many countries. Food output must be increased by raising output per acre. Two regions, North America (U.S. and Canada) and Western Europe, have less land under cultivation now than before World War II. The area under cultivation has declined for different reasons in the two regions. In Western Europe farm land has been used for roads, factories, airfields, housing, etc. In North America it has declined largely because of the acreage restrictions used to limit crop production. Both these areas can afford a decline in the area under cultivation because both are quite advanced and can raise output per acre with little difficulty. Output per acre in North America has more than doubled since the prewar period. It makes no difference to us in this country that there are no ready opportunities for greatly expanding the cultivated area. We have developed an impressive yield-raising capability.

Increasing food output by expanding the area and increasing food output by raising per-acre yields are quite different processes. Expanding the area under cultivation means simply more of the same. But increasing yields means more capital inputs; it means using fertilizer, insecticides, improved varieties, and so forth. And this is much more complicated. It requires a more sophisticated farmer. The use of very potent insecticides requires an understanding of chemistry, biochemistry, and plant physiology, and the use of fertilizer requires an understanding of the rudiments of soil fertility and plant nutrition.

The ability to raise yields has only recently developed in the United States. The frontier disappeared just before World War I, but during that war there was a great need to expand agricultural output. Prices of wheat and corn doubled and stayed at high levels for about five years. But at that time the American farmer was not yet capable of responding to these very strong incentives by increasing his output. Yields did not raise at all, and our output increased only one or two per cent each year.

In World War II we found ourselves in a similar situation: a fixed land area, a great need to increase output, rising prices beginning in 1940 and then further in 1941 and 1942. Prices were favorable and farmers responded very quickly by starting the rising yield trend that continues unabated. Yields have increased over the past twenty-five years some three per cent or more per year. At the time of World War I, our agriculture did not yet possess the level of technology and sophistication required to generate a yield takeoff.

The United Kingdom had a similar experience. During World War I the British needed more food. Prices doubled during the war, but there was little or no response on the part of farmers. In World War II, faced with a very serious domestic food situation when the foreign supplies were cut off by the U-boat menace, the farmers in the United Kingdom responded by raising yields very quickly. The United Kingdom, like the United States, apparently did not yet have the technology, the capacity, to generate a rising yield trend at the time of World War I.

The really critical question, then, as we look ahead is: "How quickly can the less developed countries make the transition from the area-expanding method of increasing food output to the yield-raising method?" What are the pre-conditions for a yield takeoff?

What about literacy? It appears that a relatively high level of literacy is a necessary but not sufficient pre-condition. A high level of literacy in itself will not generate a rapidly rising yield-per-acre trend. Stated otherwise: no major country with only a minor share of its people literate has been able to achieve a rapid increase in output per acre. Why is literacy important? In agriculture, people are widely distributed throughout the country, and the only way to disseminate new ideas rapidly is through written material. Transmitting complicated ideas to one person at a time is both costly and difficult. Farmers cannot keep farm records if they are not literate. They cannot do an input-output calculus. They cannot calculate the rate of profit. They cannot easily establish the relationship between the higher cost of improved seed planted in the spring and the change in harvest many months later.

The effort required to disseminate new ideas varies widely in countries at varying levels of development. Contrast the problems involved in getting new ideas and new techniques to farmers in the United States and in India—one society almost entirely literate and the other largely illiterate. India and the United States have about the same area of cropland—roughly 350 million acres each. The United States has four million farmers; India has sixty million. Farmers in the United States speak one language. Farmers in each of India's sixteen states speak a different language. In fact India's states are organized largely along linguistic lines.

When we want to get a new idea, a new technique, to our farmers in this country, it is fairly simple. Ideas developed in one state can be readily transmitted to farmers in other states by means of farmers' bulletins or farm magazines. And we only have to reach four million farmers, or perhaps much less because one million of our farmers account for some four-fifths of our total farm output.

We have one of the world's most efficient agricultural extension services. It is organized in each state, has representatives in each county, and its county level agricultural agents are highly trained. Many are the products of our land-grant institutions. How efficient would this same extension service be in India in view of the handicaps that exist there? Even a highly trained, highly proficient extension service might find it very difficult to accelerate greatly the rate of progress in a short time.

If literacy is so important, what does the future hold? In 1960 the United Nations estimated that fifty-one per cent of the primary school age children in Asia were in school. In Africa, it was thirty-eight per cent, and in Latin America, seventy-nine per cent. It appears that near-universal literacy for these regions is quite some distance in the future.

Another possible pre-condition is a minimal level of per-capita income. An analysis of the relationship between the level of income and the ability to raise yields in the world's major grain-producing countries is revealing. Countries were divided into three groups according to level of income: those with incomes above $1,000 per person per year; those with incomes between $200 and $1,000; and those below $200. In those countries where income was below $200 per person per year, there has been little progress in raising yield per acre over the past twenty-five years. In several countries yields actually declined. Seven of the world's major corn-producing countries have per-capita incomes below $200 per year, and in five of these countries yields were actually lower in the period from 1960 to 1962 than in the period from 1934 to 1938. In the group with incomes between $200 and $1,000, there was a mixed performance. Some showed considerable progress; others little or none. In the countries with incomes above $1,000, there were dramatic gains in yield in every case. Not one advanced country failed to raise yields impressively. In addition to being an indicator of capital availability, the level of per-capita income is also the most commonly used indicator of the level of economic development. And what we are really saying is that those countries which are more advanced have a much greater yield-raising capability than those that are not.

Another important pre-condition for a yield-per-acre takeoff is a market-oriented agriculture. In a subsistence type of agriculture, where the farmer produces for himself and his family, the output which is marketed is often just the surplus available in good crop years. In poor crop years, there is very little opportunity for getting the capital to buy the yield-raising inputs—the fertilizer, the improved seeds, and the pesticides. This capital was not required when output was being increased by expanding the area under cultivation; only a team of bullocks, a wooden plow, and some additional seed were needed. But expanding the food supply by raising output per acre requires capital to purchase the yield-raising inputs.

Another pre-condition for a yield-per-acre takeoff is a well developed nonagricultural supporting cast. This is that part of the economy outside agriculture which supplies the goods and services—ranging from fertilizers and insecticides to credit and transportation—needed to generate and to sustain a yield takeoff. Raising yields requires agricultural chemicals, machinery, and improved varieties, as well as research to develop new cultural practices. In the United States this research has been done traditionally in the experimental stations in each of our states, financed either by the state or by the federal government. In addition we have had our research program on a nation-wide basis conducted by the Agricultural Research Service of the Department of Agriculture.

Today, American industry is investing a great deal in agriculturally oriented research, to such an extent that the investment now compares favorably with that of the state and federal governments combined. This is an interesting development and perhaps one not sufficiently appreciated. The companies which sell their goods to the farmer or which buy the farmer's products are doing much of the research that underlies the progress made since World War II.

The importance of the nonagricultural supporting cast was dramatically illustrated in the Soviet Union in 1963. After suffering a serious agricultural setback, the Soviets decided that their virgin lands project had been overextended. Unable to increase output by expanding the area, it became necessary to raise per-acre yields. The Soviets then discovered that their chemical industry was not sufficiently developed to provide the agricultural chemicals needed to raise yields. And so they tried to buy fertilizer plants from West European countries and from the United States. If the Soviet Union, one of the more advanced economies, does not have the industry needed to support a rising yield trend, certainly some of the less developed countries will find it even more difficult.

Let us look at agricultural technology. The agricultural revolution, which we can define as the application of science to agriculture, began at about the same time and in the same place as the industrial revolution, namely, in northwestern Europe about two centuries ago. Most of the agricultural technology existing in the world today is in the temperate zone. But most of the less developed countries are situated in the tropics and subtropics. Even Japan, the only advanced rice economy in the world, is a temperate zone country, paralleling roughly the eastern coast of the United States from Maine to South Carolina.

Agricultural technology cannot be so readily transferred as industrial technology for many reasons. Climate is different; soils are different. A very successful variety of wheat in the United States may be a complete failure in Pakistan. A steel mill in India today uses exactly the same technology as a steel mill in Pittsburgh. The only possible difference is that the steel mill in India might be more modern, having been constructed more recently and on the basis of later technology. Industrial technology can be transferred with very little modification, but in agriculture the transfer is not so easy. Much adaptive research will be needed before the advanced agricultural techniques of the temperate zone can be modified sufficiently to be useful to farmers in the tropics.

I have used one·example by comparing India and the United States and the problems faced in agriculture. I would like to use another example to illustrate the magnitude of the problem posed by the projected increases in population in the less developed regions. Let us take the world and divide it into two parts. One is the less developed world, consisting of Asia, Africa, and Latin America, and the other is the developed world, consisting of North America, both Western and Eastern Europe, and Oceania. The population in 1960 was 850 million in the developed world, and 2.1 billion in the less developed. According to the United Nations medium level of population projections—and they now appear conservative—the population increase for the developed world between now and the end of the century is about 400 million. The increase for the less developed world is almost three billion. These two major economic regions have about the same area of land under cultivation.

Now let us exchange the projected population increases of the two regions. The developed world would then absorb the three billion increase, the less developed, the 400 million increase. And this is not unreasonable, because the developed world has the resources, while the less developed world does not. The developed world has the technology; the less developed world does not.

Now let us bring the problem closer to home. The United States accounts for about one-fourth of the developed world and would, therefore, need to absorb one-fourth of the projected increase of three billion. We would have to add, between now and the end of the century, 750 million people or about 190 million people per decade. In other words, we could expect to add the equivalent of our current population each decade from now to the end of the century. Consider what it would mean if we had to build the schools and the homes and to create the jobs for 180 million people per decade; if we had to feed this many more people while maintaining current levels of consumption. But remember that we have the advanced technology, the skills, the capital, the resources. The less developed world does not.

What then does the future look like? Can the disturbing downward trends in per-capita food production now in evidence in Asia and Latin America be reversed? Can we eliminate the widespread nutritional deficiencies found throughout the less developed regions? One thing is certain. It is going to take a much greater effort than we are currently making, a much greater effort than has ever been made before. Putting a man on the moon may be quite easy by comparison. The food-population problem as outlined here is geographically confined to the less developed regions. But we of the developed nations are equally committed to its solution.

IRENE B. TAEUBER

The Populations of the Developing Areas: Change, Transformation, and the Future

The facts of population growth in the underdeveloped areas are widely known. So also are the forebodings about the future. But a point still to be made is that in many of the areas of the world, population pressures, population growth, economic stagnation, and political instability or ineffectiveness exist in interrelations which pose urgent problems. In this amalgam of problems, comparisons and computations of the population component are often monistic. In biological analogy, human populations move like the lemmings toward an abyss of retrogression and destruction. In mathematical projection, men become so numerous that standing room only yields to layerings on the earth's surface of land and water in the multi-storied structures of some future technology. It is simple to brush aside such spectacular warnings as propagandistic and to relax in oblivion of the problems of multiplying numbers. It is neither intellectually honest nor politically safe to do so.

The imminent dangers of which we are warned are very real. In many, if not most, of the underdeveloped areas, death rates are declining while birth rates change little. Rates of population growth move upward toward maximum rates of three to four per cent a year. As these population changes occur, there is lethargy, if not retrogression, in economic and educational advance. The past can be studied; the question is the future. It is reasonable to assume that the demographic, economic, and social trends of the near future will be ordered continuations of the recent past. If so, man's increasing vulnerability is awesome even in contemplation. There are possibilities of cataclysms which dwarf any in history. The basic problem is the food to sustain life. The vaunted achievements of science, technology, technical assistance, and development activities have restored per-capita food production almost to the levels of the period before World War II. The movements of surplus grains from the United States, Canada, and Australia have averted famines in Asian countries, but the needs increase as the populations mount, and the problems of supply become more difficult. Already some half of the people have deficits and deficiencies in food so severe that malnutrition is pervasive and hunger episodic. Famine is a shadowy presence in the deliberations of national planning boards and the thinking of international organizations. It is a specter so widely perceived that the verbal Malthusianisms of only a few years ago seem unrealistic and naive.

Slowly, sometimes almost imperceptibly, men and

institutions respond to the altered balances of life and
death on this planet. Transformations proceed in the
quiet decisions of families; in the dedicated struggles of
élites in and outside government; in the studies of
scientists in the laboratories and the field; in the search
of philosophers and theologians for a reconciliation of
ancient ethical and value systems with the requirements
of a modern humanitarianism. The great transformation
now beginning is manifest in these developments, but
it is not limited to them as separable entities or as
interrelated complex. The transformation lies in the
growing knowledge that marriage, family, and reproduction are aspects of human society, whether in stability
or in change. It lies in the further knowledge that transformations in one aspect of society ramify throughout
the society. If there is one sector which is taboo, maladjustment is inherent in ongoing change, and the extent
of the maladjustment is proportionate to the centrality
of the sector which is taboo. If, therefore, there is to be
planned action, there can be no reserved sector,
particularly not one so critical as marriage, the family,
and reproduction.

The dilemma of decision for traditionalists can be
stated in categorical form. The ancient mores, institutions,
and value structures surrounding sex, the family, the
roles of women, and the relations of the generations
are aspects in a general persistence of ways of living and
working. If the institutional and the valuational bases
for human reproduction, therefore, are to remain unchanged, the people must be insulated from the intellectual currents, the material advantages, and the aroused
discontents of life outside the local areas. This means
that the death rates of the ancient order must also persist.

The price of the traditional production of life is the traditional wastage of the life which is produced.

Reduced and declining death rates are aspects of economic, social, and health developments. But they are also harbingers of demographic imbalances. The imbalances that are now manifest in increasing rates of population growth cannot continue indefinitely. Resolution may occur in either of two ways: retrogression to the high death rates of the past, or movement to the controlled birth rates of a modernizing society.

Thus the question is not whether population growth can continue indefinitely. It cannot. The question is whether declining growth will be a product of increasing death rates or declining birth rates. In broad terms, the questions concern the direction, types, speeds, and associations of movement among the demographic, economic, social, and psychological variables. The critical question is the speed of the changes which underlie reproductive behavior and the consequent rapidity with which birth rates decline to achieve again some correspondence with death rates.

Continuity in the ancient ways is not possible. Planning, operations, and changes which are to be effective involve human development in its complex totality. It is the realization of the necessity and the propriety for this involvement in human development which is the great transformation now in process.

GROWTH: FACT, ASSOCIATIONS, PROBLEMS

What has happened in human development on this earth to create the type of demographic imbalances which now exist? What are the problems of the increasing numbers?

What are the paths, the structures, and the operations which lead to socially and ethically acceptable resolutions? To answer these questions, we shall have to glance backward, outward, and forward at the broad outlines of population growth in earth's various regions. We shall use few numbers, but it is necessary to use some.

In 1900 there were less than one and one-half billion people on earth. Today there are more than three billion. In the year 2000, if present trends continue, there will be seven billion. But why, in a world of science, technology, and potentialities almost unlimited, should a five-fold increase in man's numbers be a major problem? The answer lies in the associations of growth and the areas in which growth is occurring. Today the major increases in man's numbers are those in the underdeveloped areas, not the developed ones. Numbers increase most rapidly among those least able to provide minimum subsistence for present numbers. This is a new relationship. Throughout the millenia of recorded history, growth was a response to favorable conditions, not unfavorable ones. The slow deaths by malnutrition and disease, the sudden decimations by famine and epidemic—these were the regulators of man's numbers. Today we have thrust aside much premature death. Bio-medical advances permit a control of death without a control of environment. Low death rates and high birth rates can exist alongside each other.

The present demographic crises are associated with growth rather than decline, with excessive rather than insufficient fertility. It is essential to stress the fact, therefore, that population growth itself is not an inherent problem. Nor, where growth is or has been a problem, is it always or necessarily the superfluity which constitutes the problem. The evolution of relationships between rates of reproduction and rates of dying which yield rates of change consistent with the resources base, with the state of technology, and with the dynamism in state and society is a precarious process. The totality of these relations between human reproduction, economic state, societal structure, and group persistence is not within the province of our discussion. There are three major aspects which must be noted, however, if our further considerations are to be balanced in space and temporal contexts.

In the first place, adjurations and proscriptions, folklore and philosophy, action and response reflect the population-resources-economy-society relationship in a culture at a specific time period. If it is true, as it seems to be, that all men in all cultures at most time periods have been interested in, and concerned with, their numbers and the problems of those numbers, it is also true that there has never been, nor is there now, agreement in the definition of problems. In most periods of history, the major demographic fact was the stimulation and nurture of reproductive mores which sustained reproduction and which assured survival, if not growth. The problem was decline or extinction, not increase. Given favorable conditions of living, therefore, population growth quickened, and growing numbers became a recognized problem. Prophets of doom through increase were fewer and less influential in the intellectual milieu of most periods of cultures than were the leaders whose clarion calls for increasing numbers flattered people, group, and political domain.

Second, the family institutions and the child-bearing practices of peoples have been responsive to, and interrelated components in, changes which altered ways and potentialities in living. Here we shall shift focus to our world of the twentieth century. A major sector of earth's population is now developed economically, socially, and demographically. These areas of rational relationships, if not ideal adjustment, include Europe, Russia, and Japan in Eurasia, Australia and New Zealand in Oceania and the United States and Canada in the Americas. If these areas were not already developed, they were in the process of development in the early twentieth century. There were industrializing economies, growing cities, and advancing education. Social change existed alongside economic change. Age at marriage advanced and the married limited family size. Birth rates declined along with death rates, but more swiftly, so that rates of population growth decreased. There seemed to be a natural association of birth and death rates at low as well as at high levels. Transition theory emerged along with Malthusianism as a universalist explanation. In this theory, industrialization, urbanization, and modernization, rather than the niggardliness of nature and man's propensities to reproduce geometrically, were the prime forces. With industrialization and urbanization, nations and peoples moved naturally from the slow growth or decline of high birth and death rates to the slow growth or decline of low birth and death rates.

Third, most demographers and publicists who wrote only fifteen years ago saw the major population problem as the oncoming decline of the advanced industrial and urban peoples, rather than as the continuing increase of the agrarian and rural peoples. The birth rate of the United

States had declined without major interruption from a level substantially above 50 per 1,000 total population in the late eighteenth century to a level far below 20 in the Thirties of this century. Projections into the future indicated a maximum population of 160 million in 1960, after which there would be decline. To the consternation of the demographers and in explicit violation of the regularities of history, birth rates increased to reach 25 per 1,000 total population in 1957, then wavered, with current evidences of slow declines. The rate of twenty-five was above a previously attained low, but it was only half the level of the early nineteenth century. With modern death rates, however, a birth rate of twenty to twenty-five produces appreciable population increase. The population of the United States is now more than 200 million Continuation of the levels of fertility and mortality of the recent past would give us some 300 million people within this century, some 600 million early in the twenty-first century.

And so today there are two types of areas with problems of population growth—underdeveloped areas where birth rates are unchanged and where death rates are reduced, and developed areas where birth rates have increased somewhat above previous very low levels and where death rates are very low. It is the former areas which today include most of the population of the earth and present the most difficult population problems.

POPULATION GROWTH AND POPULATION POLICIES

In the early planning of the United Nations, the Specialized Agencies, the regional associations of nations, and the United States, population growth was regarded as a lesser problem with a built-in solution. It was assumed that death rates would decline slowly with economic development, and that this development would initiate the changes which lead to declining birth rates. Any problems associated with growth would be both minimal and transitory. It was argued, therefore, that emphasis should be placed on economic and social transformations, not on population policy.

The population policy, excluded from international consideration, pertained only to the reduction of birth rates. Public health was an international and a national goal of major priority, and it was here that the great technological break-throughs occurred. Death rates could be, and were, reduced without major changes in economy or society. The scarcely conceivable thus occurred. Temporarily, and within broad limits, the associations of mortality with the conditions of living in underdeveloped areas were broken. But the association with fertility remained. Population growth moved upward to two and sometimes even three per cent or more each year. This occurred in India, Indonesia, the Philippines, Egypt, Turkey, Pakistan, Mexico, Paraguay, and Brazil. Nor are present growth rates maxima. Increases of four per cent a year already occur in some areas, and they may soon occur in others.

The impact of sharply increased rates of population growth on developmental plans and activities has been and is devastating. Absolute increases in food production have been major, but, as we have already noted, in Asia, North Africa, and Latin America, per-capita food production is lower than it was prior to World War II.

This was the precarious situation of 1964. The

balance in the coming years is likely to be even more precarious, despite the valiant efforts of the United Nations Development Decade, the FAO's Freedom-from-Hunger campaign, and this hemisphere's Alliance for Progress. The problem may be seen realistically if only India, Pakistan, and Indonesia in Asia, and Mexico and Brazil in Latin America are considered, and if the time span is limited to the years from 1960 to 1975. All persons who will be age eleven and over in 1975 are already born; actual population in 1975 can be reduced appreciably below projected ones only by increases in death rates.

In Mexico and Brazil, as in India, Pakistan, and Indonesia, populations in 1975 will be half again as large as those in 1960. Men in the productive ages will increase some fifty per cent in this fifteen year period, and this means that jobs will have to be half again as numerous merely to sustain present levels of employment, partial employment, and unemployment. The economies burdened with providing jobs for the increasing manpower will also have to provide educational facilities for a population in school ages which will be sixty per cent greater in 1975 than it was in 1960.

There are endless circles of "ifs" here. *If* there were no population growth, then savings, capital formation, and increasing production would be feasible. *If* economies were developed, capital abundant, and people skilled, there would be small families and low rates of population growth. These are both conjectures contrary to fact. The problem is twofold: (1) to achieve economic development and social change under conditions of rapid and continuing population growth; and (2) to hasten and to speed the decline in birth rates and so lessen the rate of population growth and shorten the period in which growth itself is a major deterrent to development.

This somber picture of population growth in its relations to individual welfare and national development seems somehow unreal to the government and the people of the affluent societies. It is very real in the countries facing the problems of achieving economic development and meeting the aspirations of their people while numbers increase two to three or even four per cent each year. There are policies or considerations of policies on foot in many of the countries of Asia and North Africa. The work of the United Nations Economic Commission for Asia and the Far East concentrates increasingly on the relations between population growth and economic development.

POPULATION POLICIES AND DECLINING BIRTH RATES

Developments in the programs of governments, the policy statements of international organizations, the cautious changes in the United States—these together suggest the evolution of a new intellectual climate for assessing both the problems and the prospects for population growth. The fundamental questions with which public health personnel, biologists, chemists, physiologists, and social scientists are now, and will be, concerned are those of the scientific knowledge and the technologies basic to effective organization and operation in the field of family planning. The goal is no longer that of alerting the public and the politicians, but it is the hard and prosaic task of assisting people in those changes in values and practices which replace large families with small families, high birth rates with low birth rates, rapid rates of population growth with slow rates of population growth.

The preceding paragraph was written with specific reference to the countries which have population programs, along with the United States and the international organizations. It could have been written without specificity as to country, culture, creed, or class, but it was not so written. Hence it cannot be transformed ethnocentrically into "our" problem and "our" responsibilities for the population of the earth or its major regions. Countries differ widely in their population relationships, their population growth, and the reality or the imminence of their population problems. Most seem to be moving toward the assessment of problems, the evaluation of the need for policy, the formulation of policy, and the assumption of responsibilities for family guidance as part of the responsibilities for health, development, and welfare. This is the great transformation we noted earlier.

The understanding of the present and the assessment of the future are seen most incisively in those countries where governments have already assumed responsibilities, or are currently considering responsibilities, for all aspects of population dynamics. The basic component in these new responsibilities is the sensitive one of lowered rates of reproduction. In briefest compass and in popular terminology, this is the problem of birth control.

The critical questions in the demographic process and the population future are not what governments and the press say of birth control but what intermediate operational relations there are which lead to changes in reproductive performance. This is no longer an area of ignorance in which categorical statements and verbal assaults substitute for evaluated experience. There are increasingly precise data on population, births, and deaths for increasing numbers and types of countries. There are increasing numbers of experimental programs with increasingly adequate data. There are increasingly developed methodologies for analysis and increasing sophistications in the analyses which are made. There are many broad questions to which approximate answers can be sought. As a final section and a preface to proposing a conclusion, we may note certain general results emerging from studies in many countries.

1. Birth limitation is an almost universal practice in middle-class urban groups in modernizing societies. Practices, which include the conventional contraceptives, periodic abstinence, the oral contraceptives, sterilization, and induced abortion, can be stimulated in extent and in efficiency.

2. The major problems in the underdeveloped areas lie in the villages rather than in the cities; they concern the illiterate rather than the literate, the agricultural workers rather than the professional people. The essential base for declines in national birth rates in densely settled agricultural areas is the planned limitation of births in illiterate or barely educated village populations where economic opportunities are muted and social changes are dulled.

3. The wish for a limited number of children is widespread if not universal among the women in the villages of a peasant society, whatever the indigenous culture and religion. In most societies in most time periods, this wish is neither a firm decision nor a driving motivation toward decision. Presumably women have always responded

somewhat negatively to the long vista of recurrent pregnancy and increasing burdens. This is a reasonable inference from the legend and lore concerning limitation practices that are present in most if not all societies.

4. None of the conventional means of contraception has been effective in reducing peasant birth rates in the setting of poverty, illiteracy, and hopelessness. This includes rhythm and the pill, mechanical and chemical contraceptives, and folk remedies and folk procedures.

5. The major means involved in the reduction of those birth rates which have declined swiftly in the recent past has been induced abortion, usually performed legally in health services or under government regulation outside such services. Legalization is usually rationalized on the grounds that it reduces the harmful effects of illegally induced abortion. The prevalence, the acceptability, and the efficiency of legalized induced abortion is perhaps the most somber fact in the contemporary demographic scene, whatever the continent, the region, the culture, or the religion. The countries where prevalence of the practice is associated with reduced or rapidly declining birth rates include not alone the well-known instance of Japan, but Russia, Eastern Europe, and such countries as Chile in Latin America.

6. It is not possible to envision what new means of reproductive control will become available in the near or more distant future. The intra-uterine devices now available are acceptable and effective in many cultures and to peoples of many faiths. The problem of decision-making is reduced; effectiveness is almost total for some ninety per cent of women, cost is minimal, and diffusion can extend beyond the health center.

7. Some reductions in birth rates have been achieved in limited areas. Some developing areas have declining birth

rates. Overall, however, no government policy has been organized administratively and operated effectively if the test is the reduction of the birth rate of the national population. Plans, propriety, knowledge, technologies, motivations, all are limited.

Given continuing advances in basic science, continuing improvements in technology, and continuing co-operation in international development, the problems of population growth may become present difficulties rather than limiting deterrents to advancing levels of living in developing countries. The frontiers of research may then advance to those of the values and motivations which guide and sustain individuals, families, and communities in transition to modernization.

Reduced rates of population growth are aspects of evolving solutions to the problems of economy and society; they are not themselves solutions. The problems and the tasks will remain with us for the remainder of the century but in changing forms and with changing priorities. Perhaps the surest of the predictions is that the roles and the responsibilities of the demographers and the behavioral scientists will not be antiquated in the near or even the middle future.

ALICE M. RIVLIN

Population Growth and the American Economy

Some may wonder how the economics of population growth is related to social ethics. Let me begin, therefore, by posing an ethical question—a difficult personal question which most of you will face at some time in your lives. Then we will see whether economics can throw any light on the answer.

Let us suppose that you have completed your education. A few years from now you find yourself with a good job, a nice wife and two or three children. (It does not really matter how many children you have. You face the same problem at some point.) We look in on you at a time when you and your wife are considering making a serious effort not to have any more children. The question I am raising is this: do you have any obligations to anyone besides yourselves and your present children in making this decision?

Let me be clear about the questions I am *not* posing.

I am not asking what method of family planning you should use. The choice of method is a problem for Catholics, but since I am neither a Catholic nor a medical expert I have no qualifications to discuss this choice. Let us assume that there is a method compatible with your religious convictions which you think has a reasonable chance of being successful. It does not have to be one hundred per cent successful for you to decide to try it.

I am also not raising questions about your obligations to your wife and to your present children, nor suggesting that you are poor or that you have a risky job or that you or your wife are in ill health or that you feel harassed by the responsibilities of parenthood. That would make the problem too easy. On the contrary, I have made the problem difficult by endowing you with excellent health and the financial and emotional capacity to give a good home and a good education to at least one child more than you already have. You might like to have this additional child. Would you be harming someone else by having it?

Now here, it seems to me, is a serious problem and one with which economists ought to be able to help us. Unfortunately, however, economists until now have done very little thinking along these lines. In fact, this particular problem is seldom raised in the population literature— by economists or by anyone else.

There has, of course, been concern about the economic consequences of population growth in the United States. Some viewers-with-alarm, whose contentions we will examine in a moment, paint a grim picture of what will happen if our population continues to grow at its present rate. They see America running out of resources and becoming a vast slum in which most people will have a bleaker life than they have today.

But even the viewers-with-alarm rarely see the situation as involving conflict between individual and social objectives. They often give the impression that population growth in the United States is largely due to low-income people having more children than they want or can afford. They suggest that if only the poor—especially, perhaps, the Negro and Catholic poor—would learn to limit their families to the numbers which they can support adequately, the problem would be solved. In other words, population growth is somebody else's problem. It does not involve hard decisions for middle and upper income people.

But the responsibility cannot be avoided this easily. The post-World War II baby boom cannot be attributed to the poor. Birth rates have always been high in urban slums and in low-income rural areas. This is a tragic and serious problem, but it is not a new problem. It did not cause the baby boom.

In the 1940s and 1950s, Americans from all backgrounds married in unprecedented proportions and had children at far more rapid rates than couples who married in the depression years. They did not go back to the really big families of their grandparents' time—families with seven or more children continue to decrease—but they had three children instead of two, or four instead of three, or even five instead of four. The childless marriage and the only child, which were not uncommon phenomena in the 1930s, especially among educated people, practically disappeared. We became a nation of middle-sized families. In middle and upper class suburbs as well as in city slums, the result was burgeoning schools with big classes, first in the elementary schools, then in the high schools, and now in the colleges.

I do not want to ignore the problem of high fertility among low-income groups as though I thought it were not important. There are many large families on welfare or scraping along on meager resources in cities and in poverty-stricken rural areas like parts of Appalachia. Illegitimacy rates are high—even higher than the statistics show—especially among nonwhites in urban areas. When people have children whom they do not want or whom they cannot expect to provide with food and care and shelter, the costs to society, both in resources and in human suffering, are very great.

My reason for not talking about high fertility among the poor is that I see little disagreement among thinking people, even of different religious faiths, over the objectives of public policy in this area. Clearly the objectives are to help low income people to become responsible parents; to help them to learn whatever methods are compatible with their religious convictions for planning their families sensibly, and not to have children whom they are unable to support. The dis-agreement is not over these basic objectives, but over methods of achieving them.

There is no similar consensus, however, on our first question: to what extent, in the public interest, should prosperous families limit the number of children they have? Or, to put it differently, what population policy, if any, is needed in a country in which poverty is no longer a mass problem?

Western trained economists tend to glorify freedom of choice. They contend that it is not the business of society to tell individuals what they ought to want. A good society is one in which the distribution of goods is regulated by free choice. Some things, like narcotics, have to be prohibited, but the prohibited items should be few in number and clearly dangerous to the consumer or to others. (Prohibitions are never very successful, anyway.) With these exceptions, people should be allowed to spend their incomes on the goods they want most. If they want to buy television sets instead of books, that is their privilege. A good society is one that lets them do this.

Within this framework, children can be viewed— for some purposes at least—as consumer goods. As a parent you have to choose between another child and another car or some other way of spending your income. But if you choose the child, economists who believe strongly in freedom of choice can hardly condemn your decision, unless they have strong reasons to believe that your having an additional child will be harmful to persons other than yourself. How might you be harming somebody else by making this decision in favor of the extra child?

One argument might be called the more-mouths-to-feed argument. The basic contention is that the costs of bringing up children are not borne entirely by their parents. Some costs are passed on to others.

Clearly, a society in which the birth rate suddenly shoots upward, as it did in the United States in the 1940s, faces serious problems for the first fifteen to twenty years. All these children have to be fed and clothed and educated and equipped to enter the labor force. Until they do enter

the labor force, they are not producing anything themselves. The middle-aged people have to carry the burden
and their numbers have not increased—there are more
dependents but no more workers. This can be a serious
problem—at least for a while—and it is one with which
we have some experience as a nation.

Many of the costs of rearing children, especially the
costs associated with education, are social rather than
private costs; that is, they are costs borne primarily by
the government rather than by individuals and families.
It is true, of course, that families pay taxes to support
the government, but they do not pay in proportion to the
number of children they have. Hence, it is not obvious
to an individual family that its decision to have another
child is increasing its tax burden. A family which feels
able to bear the private costs of having another child
might feel quite differently if their tax bill reflected the
full cost of the child to society as a whole.

Nevertheless, although the strain on resources
created by a sharp upturn in the birth rate may be serious,
it is temporary. The children eventually become educated.
They pass through the elementary schools into the high
schools and colleges and out into the labor force. Then
there are more workers. Unless the birth rate continues
to increase, the country is over the hump.

This is what has happened in the United States. We
ran double shifts in elementary schools in the early 1950s,
while we caught up with the demand for school rooms.
But in most places we did catch up. We are not nearly so
short of elementary school classrooms as we were a
decade ago. Now we are short of college classrooms, but
this crisis too will pass. If we build enough college

buildings to deal with the current surge of "war baby" enrollment, we will be in fairly good shape to face a continuing future inflow of roughly the same magnitude.

The more-mouths-to-feed argument, therefore, is an argument about the short-run effects of an increase in the birth rate. It does not tell us whether a sustained high birth rate is good or bad for prosperity.

The long-run effects of population increase on the level of living depend on what happens to per-capita output as the labor force increases. Population increase will lower the level of living in the long run only if per-capita output falls as the labor force increases—if, as economists say, there are diminishing returns to labor.

Most of you have undoubtedly encountered the concept of diminishing returns in an introductory course in economics. You were probably given an example involving a man with a farm of a certain acreage who works by himself with simple tools—the textbook examples always seem to be from ancient history. Maybe he gets 100 bushels of wheat from this farm. Then he finds a second man to work with him. The two-man operation is more efficient, and together they produce 300 bushels. Per-capita yield has increased. But as they add more and more people to this fixed piece of land they will eventually reach a point at which yield per man begins to diminish.

This is the classic diminishing returns example. It may be quite relevant to many underdeveloped areas today, where adding more people to fixed land and other natural resources without significant changes in technology implies lower output per man. But is it relevant to the United States?

A glance at past United States history gives little support to the notion that our economy operates under conditions of diminishing returns. On the contrary, we have absorbed tremendous numbers of people over a long period with continuing increases in per-capita output. One reason is that we have kept discovering new natural resources—more coal, more oil, more ores of various sorts. The "piece of land" in the textbook example has proved increasingly rich. A more important reason is that we have discovered more and more efficient ways of using our resources to produce higher outputs per man. Technological changes have revolutionized our whole economy every few years. Some operations, moreover, exhibit increasing rather than diminishing returns as their scale increases. Mass markets make mass production feasible and often reduce costs below what would be possible in a smaller market.

All this has been true in the past. What of the future? It is impossible to predict the course of technological change, but no one whom I know foresees a slowdown in the rate of technological progress of productivity per man. On the contrary, many people are alarmed by the rapid pace of recent technological advances. They are worried that we will soon be able to produce so much with so little labor that even with rapidly rising output most people will have nothing to do. I do not share this worry, but I certainly see no prospect of productivity decline. The specter of diminishing returns does not haunt the United States for the foreseeable future.

Let me pause for a moment to consider a counter argument which has been advanced by some economists: that rapid population growth in a developed country is actually necessary to prevent economic stagnation due to inadequate investment opportunities.

This argument—often called the stagnation thesis— is associated with the name of the distinguished economist, Alvin Hansen, who first advanced the thesis in a presidential address to the American Economic Association in the late 1930s and stirred up a lively controversy which lasted into the postwar period.

The stagnation thesis was bound up with the new economic thinking of John Maynard Keynes. In simplified form it went something like this: individuals and families normally spend most of their incomes. This spending creates a demand for goods and services. Spending by one person becomes income to someone else. But people do not spend *all* their income. The part which is saved is subtracted from the income stream. It does not create a demand for goods and services or become income to other people. Hence, the fact that some income is saved will mean less aggregate income in the future unless enough investment takes place to fill the gap. We cannot be sure that enough investment opportunities will exist to provide an outlet for desired saving, but one thing which clearly creates a high inclination to invest is rapid population growth.

If population is increasing rapidly, a high level of investment becomes almost a necessity. Communities have to build schools and hospitals and roads, and private construction and other investment will also be high. If population is growing slowly or not at all, people may get along fairly well by simply repairing and occasionally replacing the buildings and equipment they already have. The stagnationists pointed out that the slow-down in population growth in the 1930s provided at least a partial explanation of the lagging investment and high unemployment of the Great Depression.

The pros and cons of the stagnation thesis are of mainly historical interest and need not detain us here. The important point, I think, is that even if we accept the stagnation thesis as a partial explanation of the Great Depression, it does not follow that maintaining a high rate of population growth is a sensible way of filling the investment gap. Having babies to stimulate investment is about as rational as having a big defense establishment solely to maintain full employment. It is true that government spending on tanks, guns, and rockets creates employment, but employment can also be created by spending for items which are useful in themselves or, at least, not dangerous. Similarly, the investment gap—if it exists—can be filled in more sensible ways than by producing otherwise unwanted children.

So far, we have not found a convincing reason for viewing long-run population growth as either favorable or unfavorable to the economic well-being of Americans. But maybe we have not found the right ways to measure well-being. We have been assuming, at least implicitly, that well-being is measured by goods and services per capita—perhaps, net national product divided by the population.

Incidentally, some people talk as though the right measure of national economic success is simply aggregate output of goods and services; they even forget to put in the "per capita." This is surprising, but it really happens. Much of the discussion of growth rates—including the famous "growth-manship" comparisons between Russia and America a few years ago—has been stated in terms of national product without reference to population size. (One might as well say that the Chinese are better off than the Dutch because they have a higher gross national product.)

Clearly, we have to get the population size in somewhere. But even if we do—even if we think in terms of net national product per capita—are we measuring the right things?

Much of what goes into the quality of life is not reflected in statistics or quantitative outputs. The sun and the moon, the mountains and the beach, pure air and clean water, for example, do not get into national product measures. Neither do values like privacy and quiet and freedom from traffic jams. Many vitally important things are missed altogether.

I think economists will have to focus on these missing items if they are going to tell us anything useful about the way in which population growth is likely to affect future well-being in the United States. In underdeveloped areas it is not necessary to be so fancy. In India or Egypt, for example, it is clear that a drop in the population growth rate would make economic development much easier. In the United States, on the other hand, it seems likely that present rates of population increase could be maintained for a long time without lowering per-capita national product as it is conventionally measured.

But what about the unmeasured items? Can we say anything about them?

This is the point at which most economists used to give up, but they do not give up so easily any more.

People keep asking hard questions such as: how much should the government spend for parks and recreation? To help answer this kind of question economists have had to try to put values on things like recreation or enjoying the outdoors.

Valuing recreation is not just a theoretical exercise. It affects real decisions. Suppose that the government is considering a big water resource project. The costs of the project can be estimated and some of the benefits may not be hard to measure—the value of electricity to be produced, the anticipated savings from flood control and so forth. But if these measurements leave the decision in doubt someone is sure to say, "What about those lakes? Are not swimming and boating and fishing and beautiful picnic places worth something to the taxpayer?" Clearly, they are, but how much?

Economists often try to handle this kind of question by estimating how much people would be willing to pay for the use of a recreational facility if it were available—how far would they travel to get there and what level of entrance fee would they pay? Some of the same techniques might be used to make estimates of the values people place on privacy and space and ease of commuting.

In many instances the value people attach to privacy in this country does not seem to the casual observer to be especially high. My family and I recently drove to a beach on Chesapeake Bay. There was a small area of the beach where hot dogs and soft drinks were sold. Everyone was jammed in right there, one next to the other. It was only necessary to walk a few yards down the beach to get away from the crowd, but hardly anyone besides ourselves took the trouble to do this. I doubt if five per cent of those present would have paid a quarter to be on a less crowded beach!

It is easy to become confused between the question of aggregate population size and the question of population concentration in small areas. Some of those who are alarmed about the rate of population growth in the United States point to the ugly, crowded conditions of our cities and suggest that lowering the birth rate is a solution to these ills. They forget that people have been streaming into the cities from outlying areas in tremendous numbers. Many rural sections of the country have been losing population. We would have had congestion in the cities even without the "baby boom."

Of course cities do not have to be ugly; they can be planned with space and trees, imaginative architecture and convenient shopping areas. Old cities can be rebuilt and new ones can be created. As an alternative to doubling the size of Chicago, perhaps we should consider building a new city the size of Chicago in Wyoming. This would be expensive, but it would not be irrational for a productive society which puts a high value on children and on urban living simply to accept the cost of rebuilding old cities and building new ones in Wyoming. The alternatives merit serious consideration.

Finally, there is the question of implementing a population policy, once we have one. Suppose that we have carefully considered all the tangible and intangible costs and benefits of population increase and that we have become convinced that the present rate of increase is too high. We believe that families are not considering the full costs to the community by adding more children to it, and that the future well-being of the population would be enhanced by a lower growth rate. What should we do about it?

I am still not raising the question of what methods of family planning should be used. Suppose everybody plans their families, but everybody wants four children and this means that the population doubles every generation. If we think this rate of increase is too high, how do we convince people to want fewer children?

The standard answer is: education and persuasion. This might work and it certainly should be tried first. There are prosperous countries in the world with far lower birth rates than our own, and we might learn something from them. Why do Swedish families, for example, apparently want fewer children than American families want?

Education and persuasion, however, are not always effective in convincing people not to buy things they want and can afford. If education and persuasion fail, what then? A real dilemma arises here, because it is difficult to treat children as ordinary consumers' goods for the purpose of convincing families not to "buy" them. The purchase of ordinary consumer goods can be discouraged by making them more expensive. In the case of cars, for example, the costs to the community of individual car ownership are very great. Streets and roads, bridges, parking facilities, and traffic control are all expensive. In theory at least, these social costs can be shifted onto the car owner through taxes on the ownership and operation of his car. This makes it more expensive to own a car and discourages some people from doing so.

The difficulty is that the social costs of having children cannot be shifted onto families without penalizing the children themselves. This basic dilemma arises in connection with welfare programs. It is hard, for example, to devise a public program which will discourage illegitimacy without penalizing illegitimate children once they are born. The difficulties would be intensified if we moved in the direction of shifting the full cost of education onto families. Many families would undoubtedly choose to have fewer children if they had to pay for their education, but the children of low-income families would be at an even greater disadvantage than they are today. I do not know the solution to this dilemma, but it deserves earnest thought.

JOHN L. THOMAS

Issues, Facts, and Population
Policy Re-Examined

Despite the necessarily hypothetical character of past
population estimates and the admitted inadequacy of
most contemporary statistics, it is becoming increasingly
clear that the population of the world has begun to grow
at an unprecedented rate and possesses the potential of
even faster development. Thus, although world population
is variously estimated to have reached only between 470
and 545 millions by 1650, it had tripled in size by 1900
and has now climbed to roughly 3 billion.

Since there is little evidence for assuming widespread
differences in natural fecundity or the ability to procreate,
it seems clear that the traditional checks of disease,
famine, and war no longer serve as effective controls on
rapid population growth. The profound implications of
this change have been partially obscured among the
industrialized nations of the West because extensive
use of contraceptive techniques, sterilization, and

abortion has led to a drastic reduction in their birth rates. Although such means must be regarded as ethically objectionable, the fact that they effectively checked rapid population growth leads most social scientists and moral philosophers to ignore the real significance of what had happened.

Today we must face the fact that, like all other living species, the human race possesses a considerable procreative capacity. If this reproductive potential is fully actualized, or if death resulting from disease, famine, and war does not eliminate a fair percentage of men before they can reproduce, human population will grow rapidly. At present the large agrarian societies of the world, including roughly two-thirds of the current human population, are apparently procreating at near capacity levels, while the widespread application of modern health techniques developed in the industrialized West is rapidly lowering the death rates, primarily through control of the infectious diseases that formerly eliminated large numbers of infants and children. Inasmuch as this rapidly increasing two-thirds of the world's population lives in countries producing only one-third of the world's food and even less of its industrial wealth, it is not surprising that programs designed to promote economic development are usually accompanied by proposals to curb the birth rates.

Although our interest in helping the economically lesser-developed countries solve their growing problems is obviously well placed, it is highly regrettable that this concern has tended to obscure the significant fact that, judged from the viewpoint of Catholic moral standards, the fundamental issues relating to population control are essentially the same for all modern nations. Granted present nuptiality rates, age at marriage, and advances in health care, no modern country can long make reasonable provision for its population increases unless a good percentage of its fertile couples take effective steps to regulate family size. With the possible exception of Ireland, the problem of population control has not received a moral solution among the developed nations of the West, and realism demands that we keep this fact in mind when discussing the Catholic position on the current world situation.

Because most of us are not yet accustomed to living in a statistically comprehensible world, we may find it difficult to grasp the revolutionary character of the changes that have occurred. Our sudden confrontation with global population statistics is bound to generate some emotional strain. Many of our traditional conceptions and trusted views are being called into question. Yet the peculiar nature of the problem leaves us few avenues of escape, for we can feel its impact at many different levels. Not only our recent emergence as the dominant power in the free world and our consequent awareness of the plight of the economically under-developed Third World, but also our belated recognition of the extent of poverty amid affluence in The Other America, as well as our mounting apprehension regarding the results of automation, an expanding work-force, and integration, serve to remind us that serious population problems exist both at home and abroad. We can no longer afford to be ignorant of the facts.

Baffling global statistics, however, are not the only disturbing items in the picture. Population problems

are related to human sexuality, and changes affecting
sex necessarily call into question the beliefs, values, and
norms of conduct traditionally associated with its morally
and socially acceptable expressions. Neither primitive
nor culturally advanced societies have ever displayed
marked ability for dealing rationally with sex. As a result,
most discussions involving conflicting viewpoints on
sexuality, perhaps even more than similar discussions
relating to religion or politics, tend to be characterized
by unacknowledged emotional biases rather than by
balanced judgments.

Considering the complexity and radical implications
of current population trends, I feel that the conceptual
grasp of the situation, requisite for formulating adequate
policy, must include knowledge of the basic factors
affecting population growth, together with some understanding of the nature of human sexuality and the systems
of control found workable in the past. Hence, after
describing the new dimensions of the present situation, I
shall proceed to discuss the relevant factors in each of
these areas. This approach is based on the conviction that
most current programs for dealing with the problems are
patently inadequate because they are too limited in scope.
For the most part, contemporary proposals tend to be
polarized around two opposite extremes. On the one
hand, we find those who would avoid facing the main
issues by trusting to some vague type of providentialism
or believing that some as yet unknown regulatory
mechanisms in the human species will come into operation
ultimately to slow down deleterious population growth.
On the other, are those who would ignore the complexities
of the real situation and anxiously advocate various types

of short-range programs designed to lower presently high
birth rates quickly and at all costs.

THE NEW DIMENSIONS OF THE SITUATION

Both these general approaches proceed on the implicit
assumption that the contemporary situation regarding
population is qualitatively similar to the past. All that
has changed is our awareness of the problems and their
increasing magnitude. It should be clear, however, that
reproductive and parental attitudes and practices
consonant with the high infant mortality rates and
relatively simple, technologically undeveloped social
organizations of the past are no longer compatible with
the present human condition, at least in contemporary
Western societies. Programs that ignore this fact, while
placing primary emphasis either on maximizing the use
of natural resources or inhibiting the normal outcome
of human procreative activity, merely postpone the date
of eventual confrontation with the real situation.

The specifically new dimensions of the population
problem may be stated briefly as follows. Since concern
with reproduction, considered in terms of both individual
fulfillment and social continuity, constitutes one of the
major wellsprings of organization and motivation in all
human societies, changes radically affecting man's
relationship to reproduction will have profound repercussions on his total conduct of life and, consequently,
will require serious rethinking and restructuring of all
relevant human relationships. But beginning around the
sixteenth century a series of developments in science,
industry, medicine, and other areas, together with the

introduction of radical new thought-ways in philosophy and theology, so modified traditional attitudes and practices relating to standards of living, infant and maternal health care, social mobility, the status of women, and the formal education of children, that the nature of man's traditional relationship to reproduction gradually underwent qualitative changes. It is precisely the far-reaching individual and institutional implications of modern man's changed relationship to reproduction which constitute the specifically new dimensions in the present situation.

In other words, if our hypothesis regarding the crucial significance of man's concern with reproduction is substantially correct, contemporary population problems are not merely old problems magnified or dressed up in modern statistical trappings, but are qualitatively different problems stemming from markedly different sources and requiring new frames of value referents for their solutions. To be sure, the imbalance between rapidly expanding numbers and underdeveloped natural resources currently existing in many large sections of the world constitutes an immediate challenge that cannot be ignored, but Western man has already clearly demonstrated that he is quite capable of family limitation and wasteful overproduction. Hence, although the search for more reliable and acceptable means of population control, as well as for better methods of exploiting natural resources, must continue unabated, success in this pursuit alone will solve no fundamental human issues.

Briefly, modern man's changed status in regard to reproduction requires a thorough reinterpretation of the personal and social significance of human sexuality, together with an integrated, consistent reformulation of the manifold relationships relevant to its meaningful development, expression, and regulation under current conditions. The restricted procreation and limited family size now being practiced and more or less universally required in the foreseeable future raise serious questions regarding the essential relationship between sex and procreation, the function of non-procreative marital relations in maintaining the unity of the monogamous couple, attitudes and practices regarding parenthood, the ambivalence of woman's role under conditions of limited motherhood, the implications of small family size for parental roles, the balanced development of children, and so on.

These questions remain largely unexamined, though there is increasing evidence of frustration, normlessness, and growing incapacity to find more than passing significance in the personally and socially crucial area of sexual relations. Several elements in the historical development of family limitation in Western society go far toward explaining this lack of concern with basic issues. The initial rapid diffusion and widespread acceptance of birth control practices occurred for the most part, particularly in France and the United States, without benefit of clergy, enlightened *philosophes*, or well-organized propaganda. This suggests that although the traditional interpretations of sexuality were not capable of supplying a meaningful moral framework within which effective ways of meeting the changed exigencies of reproduction under modern conditions could be developed, this fact was ignored by both religious and secular leaders alike. When individual couples took matters into their own hands as the increasing pressure of circumstances generated effective desire to limit family size, their actions were publicly condemned, even though no workable alternatives were provided, and the far-reaching consequences of what was happening attracted no serious attention.

As we have pointed out, there is need for a thorough reinterpretation of the personal and social significance of human sexuality, as well as for a thoughtful restructuring of the various relationships relevant to its meaningful development, expression, and regulation. This approach would include the careful formulation of an integrated view of human sexuality, a view that would take into account not only the complementary character of its physiological, psychological, and spiritual attributes, together with the various stages of sexual growth in the process of personality development, but also the individual and institutional implications of its function as a unique means of expressing human love and creativity. Religion and philosophy, as well as the various medical and social sciences, must make their contributions to the formulation of this integrated view—no single discipline is adequate for dealing with the complex phenomena involved.

MAJOR FACTORS INFLUENCING BIRTH RATES

What are some of the basic facts we must keep in mind when considering population policy? There is general agreement in every enduring society that the institution of marriage should normally provide for the continuity or conservation of the group in time. Effective provision for continuity in this regard obviously implies the adequate procreation and education of offspring; while these processes, in turn, are affected by current fertility and death rates, by the type of social organization maintained by the group, and by prevailing beliefs, attitudes, and practices regarding marriage and parenthood. Each of these variables merits further examination.

First of all, we may consider the factors directly influencing fertility. Of prime importance among these, of course, is the inherent capacity to procreate, which includes both the reproductive organs and the various sexual impulses or drives normally inclining individuals to engage in marital relations. This capacity varies with individuals, individual couples, and especially with age, for the reproductive span in women is definitely delimited by the menarche and menopause. Although reproductive capacity may differ considerably among individuals, it appears, from what evidence is now available, that it does not differ significantly among the various nations of the Western world considered as a whole.

The fertility rate of a given group is also affected by the frequency of exposure to pregnancy. This is related to the frequency of intercourse in marriage, the average age at marriage, the proportion of members who never marry, and the extent of the reproductive period spent after or between unions when marriages are broken by divorce, desertion, or death. Further, involuntary abstinence from marital relations due to impotence, illness, or forced separation; from involuntary infecundity or sterility; from involuntary foetal mortality (reproductive wastage) when pregnancies terminate in miscarriages, abortions, or stillbirths; and above all, from the extent and effectiveness with which various types of voluntary birth control may be employed, are significant factors directly affecting fertility.

In the second place, since man is a social being, the factors mentioned above are themselves affected by the conditions and circumstances of organized group life. Among other indirect influences, we might mention the culturally determined customary age at marriage, the amount and quality of education required for adequate participation in society, the way the family makes its living, and the general physical and mental health of the reproductive members of the group. As we may learn from the study of different cultures, some family systems, as well as various social or religious laws and customs, may exert considerable influence on the fertility of a group by regulating the requirements for entrance into marriage and the pattern of marital relations within marriage.

Third, because man is endowed with reason, he uniformly seeks to discover the natures and purposes of things and to regulate his conduct accordingly. As a result, human fertility tends to be affected not only by the innate capacity to reproduce and the social circumstances within which reproduction is carried out, but also by the way various groups define the natures and purposes of sex, marriage, and parenthood, together with the patterns of conduct they judge acceptable to achieve their objectives in this regard. In all societies, decisions relating to fertility are strongly affected by the group's value system, which tends to define both the goals worth striving for and the means used to attain them.

Finally, the continuity of a given group does not depend solely on the above factors. The prevailing death rate is of supreme importance. This depends on man's innate capacity to survive to a certain age, on his ability to provide food, shelter, clothing, health care, and protection from enemies, and on his attitudes toward suffering, sickness, and death. The extent to which death eliminates individuals before or during their primary reproductive periods is particularly pertinent, for a high death rate among such age groups requires a correspondingly high birth rate to maintain a stable population.

The continuity of a given group, therefore, ultimately depends on the type of relationship maintained between birth and death rates. If the death rate is high, as it still is in some sections of South America, Africa, and the Orient, and as it was among Western nations until after the middle of the seventeenth century, nearly the full capacity to reproduce must be exercised by the group in order to maintain a stationary or slowly increasing population. On the other hand, if the death rate drops rapidly, as it is doing in the large agrarian societies of the world through the widespread application of modern health techniques developed in the industrialized West, and if the birth rate continues to be high, a rapid growth in population will result. Such disparity between birth and death rates has minor, overall significance when it occurs among relatively small population groups, yet even a moderately favorable shift in the ratio between births and deaths in large nations like China, India, the Soviet Union, or the United States produces very sizable annual increments.

THE NATURE OF HUMAN SEXUALITY

As we have suggested, one of the emotionally disturbing elements inherent in population problems is the fact that they are necessarily related to human sexuality, and mankind has always been somewhat ill at ease in dealing with human sexual phenomena. Historically, cultural reactions have run the gamut from severe repression to relative permissiveness. Although a rejecting Manichaean strain has run through all Western Christian societies, this has apparently always been accompanied by an opposite tendency to regard sex as a kind of perennial, providential seven-year-itch to be exploited for pleasure and profit. At the present time there is special need to develop an adequately comprehensive view of human sexuality since there is widespread confusion, uncertainty, and doubt regarding the relevance of the sexual values and norms traditionally fostered by the Judaic and Christian faiths.

Sex has such far-reaching consequences for both men and women because it involves the possession of a generative system that is incomplete and consequently requires the cooperation of an "other" sex if it is to be fulfilled. Considered from the viewpoint of the individual person, sex constitutes a way both of being-to-the-world and being-to-others. As a way of being-to-the-world, it affects all levels of an individual's activity: psycho-physical, psycho-social, and spiritual. As a way of being-to-others, it is reflected in the sexually determined, culturally defined statuses and roles in terms of which boys and girls are trained and which later determine their relative social positions, acceptable areas of activity and permitted aspirations or goals in the adult community.

Sex also has significant implications for society or the human group, for it constitutes the natural basis for marriage and the family. Hence society is concerned with sex because it constitutes the foundation of that primary human community of life and love designed to provide for the orderly fulfillment of the couple's sexually related needs and to guarantee the adequate procreation and education of new members of society.

According to the presently available knowledge concerning the major motivational systems in man, the central neural mechanisms controlling his sexual responses are not dependent on physiological maturation or seasonal physiological changes in his endocrine glands as in most animals. Moreover, even when sexually aroused, his sexual goal behavior is not innate or "built-in" but is the product of learning; and this goes far toward explaining the great variety of sexual practices and so-called sexual perversions characterizing human sexual activity. These facts have an important bearing on problems of population control. The absence of a sexual instinct in man, in the sense that he inherits no innate desire to attain any specific behavioral goals in this regard, strongly underlines the significance of culturally defined sexual values and practices, as well as the need for adequate sex education and the internalizing of appropriate controls. At the same time, the fact that the neural mechanisms controlling his sexual responses are not dependent on physiological developments in his endocrine system considerably enlarges the scope of his freedom and responsibility.

One further characteristic of human sexuality merits

mention in terms of our present purposes. Although the reproductively mature human female is capable of conceiving during only a relatively brief period in each menstrual cycle, the human couple have no direct knowledge of the precise time of ovulation and remain sexually responsive and receptive throughout the entire cycle. In other words, the human female does not experience the typical mammalian seasonal or cyclical oestrus during which period alone she is sexually receptive, nor does human intercourse induce ovulation, as sexual congress does among some animals.

This suggests that it is the entire marital process of sexual relations rather than the individual act of intercourse that should be regarded as procreative, and that this on-going process is designed to fulfill not only a reproductive but a unifying function in normal marriages. Hence when fertile couples are permitted to control the procreative potential of this process only through the observance of absolute or periodic continence, they must also sacrifice the benefits of its unifying or relational function. Since the principles and norms governing marital chastity were developed at a time when the cyclical nature of ovulation was unknown and the unifying relational function of the process was largely ignored, many now feel that these traditional principles and norms are no longer relevant and must be revised.

SYSTEMS OF SEXUAL CONTROL

Because the contemporary emphasis on the merely genital aspects of sexuality tends to obscure the basic relationship between sex and procreation, most current policy proposals fail to consider problems of population control within the wider context of prevailing systems of sexual control. Yet it should be obvious that culturally determined attitudes and practices relating to the expressions of sex may either excessively stimulate the sexual needs of a group, pervert them, harmfully repress them, or channel them into personally and socially developmental patterns. Considered from the viewpoint of individual couples and society, sex does derive its essential significance from its relationship to procreation. Hence the mere discovery of facile means for controlling conception does not in itself confer meaning on marital relations but, as we have indicated, gives rise to a whole new series of problems.

History reveals that all enduring human societies have had to establish some system of sexual control lest the uninhibited individual expressions of sex result in activities considered disruptive of the social order. The formulation of workable controls has always been difficult. Considering the complexity of the personal and social variables involved and the various ways that groups may define human nature and its sexual needs, it is not surprising that cultures differ greatly in the way in which they have defined their prohibitions and permissions.

Moreover, as British anthropologist J. D. Unwin pointed out in *Sex and Culture*, an exhaustive review of all the pertinent cross-cultural data available leads to the conclusion that no known culture has ever developed or maintained an advanced state of civilization without enforcing relatively strict sexual controls. All such sexual controls have their "costs," for their effective implementation involves definite functional exigencies in terms of social conditions, the formation of appropriate attitudes, and the structuring of cross-sex associations throughout the entire life-cycle.

In general, mankind has followed two well-defined approaches in formulating systems of sexual control. The first is society-centered and does not seek to regulate individual expressions of sex directly. Hence it regards sexual phenomena from the viewpoint of society rather than from the viewpoint of the person. Because control is needed to maintain society's marriage, reproductive, kinship, status, and ceremonial systems, regulations are established in terms of the exigencies of these systems. Outside the regulated areas, each individual is permitted free sexual expression. In other words, sexual conduct in itself is regarded as nonmoral; one "sins" only when his action violates certain socially established patterns. This approach is common to most cultures outside the Judaic and Christian spheres of influence.

The second approach is person-centered and focuses on the conscious expression of sex itself. Hence it seeks to establish norms of control covering all manifestations of sex under all circumstances. This is the characteristic Judaic and Christian personalist approach, which considers sex primarily from the viewpoint of the individual and weighs the consequences of its use or misuse in terms of the perfection of the person. This does not imply that social consequences are ignored, but norms of control are formulated in terms of each person's responsibility for the right use of his faculties. In practice, therefore, controls in this approach will appear to focus on the sexual drive itself rather than on those specific expressions of sex that the group may consider particularly disruptive of good order.

Although the point of departure and return in this latter approach is the human person, not society, it is the person integrally conceived. This means that the person is conceived as capable of arriving at an objective norm of morality, as morally responsible for his conduct, and as possessing a transcendental life-goal or destiny. Considered in terms of this transcendental goal, all other values are regarded as intermediate ends or means. The adequate development of personality and full self-realization are evaluated in terms of the development and self-realization of the whole person. Specifically, expressions of sex are regarded as developmental only to the extent that they conform to the nature and destiny of the integral person.

Both person-centered and society-centered approaches produce sets of culturally standardized sexual codes ranging through definitely prescribed, preferred, or permitted patterns of behavior to those definitely proscribed. Both solve the problem of reconciling the need for control with the need of expression; in each approach, however, solutions are based on different premises of values. As participants of the broad stream of Western culture, the American people have tended to take the person-centered approach to sexual controls, yet it is becoming increasingly evident that large numbers no longer accept the philosophical and theological principles upon which this approach is ultimately founded. This growing moral pluralism also destroys the consensus needed to develop a society-centered approach, with the result that contemporary society lacks any recognizable, uniform system of sexual control.

Accordingly, much of the confusion concerning sexual morality today stems from the fact that traditional, and still officially approved, values, standards, and norms were derived from a conception of the person which is no longer accepted by some and which is no longer clearly recognized by many others as the only logical basis of the codes which they desire to maintain. More important, the rejection of the philosophical and theological principles in terms of which the personalist approach was formulated has not only destroyed the foundation of traditional values and controls but has deprived the American people of a common, shared conceptual framework of values within which they could formulate the new system of controls required by contemporary social conditions.

CONCLUSION

Because population trends requiring programs of control are necessarily related to the cultural and social environments within which they occur, attempts to formulate a uniform, overall population policy for the future appear quite unrealistic. The actual dimensions of the Malthusian dilemma still differ widely from region to region, and practical population policies must be formulated accordingly. Hence, although I have insisted that the essential source of the current problem is man's changed relationship to reproduction, since the radical implications of this change become apparent only when countries reach a certain general level of economic development, there is need to formulate short-range programs designed to meet the immediate problems currently experienced in transitional societies.

Briefly, in formulating such programs we must keep in mind that, inasmuch as functioning social systems are integrated, gradual, or piecemeal, reforms such as family limitation offer no solution to existing population problems. People can live with reasonable satisfaction in an "archaic" peasant society or in an "adapted" industrialized urban environment, but not in any half-way house. In other words, when death rates are rapidly lowered by the introduction of alien techniques and practices which do not affect the traditional social and economic situations of underdeveloped countries, these societies must choose between immediate conversion to an intensive industrial development or increasing poverty and decline. Piecemeal reforms such as birth control are ineffective both because they are not aimed at changing traditional social and economic conditions and because they cannot prove feasible until such changes occur.

Thus the crux of the immediate problem we face here is how to promote the cultural transition required if people of underdeveloped countries are to be converted to rapid industrial development. There are no facile solutions. Administrative measures, institutional and economic policy changes, and social means in both resource-adequate and resource-needy countries must be developed if we are to meet the challenge effectively. Given our dominant position in the free world, it is essential that we labor under no misconceptions concerning the difficulties of the problem or the complex character of its solution.

Finally, to return to the central population issues in the Western world, there is need to develop a philosophy of human sexuality that will take into consideration modern man's changed relationship to reproduction and which will give due weight to both the unifying and procreational aspects of marital relations. Since it is inconceivable that couples in any advanced industrial society will return to unrestricted procreation, the personal and social implications of widespread conception control and small family size must be carefully studied. Although the relationship between sex and procreation has been profoundly modified, in the final analysis sexual relations still derive their objective significance from this relationship, and this fact must serve as a guiding principle in reconstructing a system of sexual controls capable of inculcating the disciplined self-restraint required for the mature expression of sex under modern social conditions.

JOHN L. THOMAS

Population Control and the
Catholic Family

Most adult Americans are quite aware that traditional attitudes and practices relating to sex, marriage, and family life have been profoundly affected by our rapid transition to an industrialized urban society. Yet the majority appear strangely unperturbed by what has happened. Concern with the long-range implications of these changes has received only passing attention in the relaxed atmosphere of our affluent society. Following a policy of "buy now and pay later," young American couples enter marriage and start their families with unquestioning faith in their personal resources and the continued stability of our economic system. Perhaps any society of abundance tends to focus attention on the affective, short-range, ephemeral aspects of life, yet contemporary American couples appear excessively oriented toward the immediate and the local, displaying a kind of permanent immaturity in their lack of concern regarding future contingencies or even fairly obvious consequences.

Under these circumstances, it is not surprising that, until the last several years, population problems have attracted only spasmodic, segmented, and rather super-ficial attention. Owing to the remarkable reduction of marriage and birth rates occurring during the depression years of the Thirties, most social scientists hastily assumed that the nation's period of rapid native growth had come to an end. Short of extensive immigration, our population would increase slowly, if at all, and the major focus of demographic concern became the disparity of reproductive rates among the various social classes. Hence the reversal of trends, indicated by the postwar "baby boom," was initially misinterpreted as a passing phase, while the nation's sudden involvement in inter-national affairs quickly shifted the major focus of both expert and popular attention to the startling population increases among the economically underdeveloped two-thirds of the world.

Judging from the currently expanding volume of writing and discussion relating to population control, we may safely conclude that most Americans are begin-ning to acquire some awareness that significant new problems exist. There is little indication, however, of widespread understanding that the complexity and multiplicity of the factors involved, together with our present ignorance of many relevant facts, preclude all facile solutions. Population problems are inherently related to the very foundations of human organization and motivation. Changes affecting man's concern with reproduction have profound repercussions on the total conduct of life. Voluntary methods of population control become operative only when there is adequate motivation, and such motivation requires that couples regard control as feasible in terms not only of their material and social resources but also of cherished life-values.

Writing shortly before the outbreak of World War II, Swedish child psychologist and population expert, Alva Myrdal, predicted with remarkable insight that the population problem would become the dominant political issue of the future, an issue that would be discussed "in the folk-parliaments of street, workshop, and family circle as well as in the parliaments of states and in the conferences of economists, sociologists, and biologists." Today we are witnessing the fulfillment of her prediction, although a series of scientific developments, the subsequent accumulation of a mass of global statistics, and the introduction of conflicting ideological positions have vastly extended the scope of discussion and further obscured the relevant issues. Hence it is no easy matter to maintain critical balance and objectivity when dealing with the emotion-loaded, frequently propaganda-inflated problems associated with current world population trends. Perhaps in dealing with no other issues are modern Catholics in particular made more sharply aware that they are members of a religious minority that cherishes a distinctive value system in a curiously permissive, morally pluralist society.

THE SCOPE OF THE PRESENT DISCUSSION

We are not directly concerned here, however, with the broader, overall problems associated with contemporary world populations trends. Our aim is somewhat restricted, in the sense that we shall discuss some of the more immediate problems which individual Catholic couples may face in regulating the size of their families under contemporary conditions. Human sexual desires and needs are not automatically regulated either by the demands of marital love or the parental abilities of the couple. Owing to a series of social changes and developments, it is becoming clear that many Catholic couples are finding it increasingly difficult to reconcile the normal expressions of their love with the requirements of the moral law. Since change is inherent in every society and family life is necessarily affected by the social and cultural contexts within which it develops, each generation of couples must face somewhat different challenges in this regard. The family problems of contemporary couples will differ from those faced by their parents, though the ultimate goal of striving for mutual happiness and sanctity remains the same for all generations of Catholic couples.

Stated briefly, remarkable advances in health care, accompanied by rapid changes in our social system and marriage patterns, have profoundly modified traditional responsibilities, attitudes, and practices relating to the bearing and rearing of children. Throughout much of the past it was generally assumed that average couples were able to bear and rear all the children whom they might be privileged to have throughout the course of their marriage, though the long history of contraception, sterilization, abortion, and infanticide also suggests that there have always been some individuals who for various reasons have attempted to frustrate or eliminate the normal outcome of sexual relations. At the present time, however, owing to early age at marriage, extensive emphasis on sexual stimulation and expression, high standards of maternal and infant health care, and added length of formal training required to prepare children for adequate participation in a technologically advanced society, most fertile young couples are faced with the serious challenge of spacing pregnancies and regulating the size of their families.

In our morally pluralist society, moreover, Catholic couples must solve their family problems within a framework of beliefs, values, and norms no longer recognized as valid by most of their contemporaries. This means that as members of a religious minority they must work out their salvation within a social system geared to the small family and operating on the assumption that contraceptive birth control will be extensively employed. Since this key-solution is unacceptable to Catholic couples, the entire web of their marital and family relationships must be structured accordingly.

In other words, because they cherish a distinctive system of values and live in a morally pluralist society characterized by rapid and extensive change, American Catholic couples face a number of family problems not shared by their contemporaries. The special social pressures which Catholic families experience in modern society are directly related to the family ideals and standards which they seek to realize in their lives. Together with all other couples, Catholics must make continuous adjustments and adaptations in meeting their changing social situations, but their choice of suitable modes of conduct will necessarily be limited by their Christian philosophy of life. The radical implications of this limitation of choice are frequently underestimated because the relatively complete secularization of family values in American society has proceeded largely unnoticed. Hence considering the aim of the present discussion, a more detailed analysis of the relevant factors in the current situation may prove helpful.

THE CATHOLIC DESIGN FOR MARRIAGE

Owing to the Church's longstanding concern with the sacrament of matrimony, as clearly manifested in the historical developments of her dogma, moral theology, and canon law, Catholic teaching relating to marriage and the family is now expressed in a unified, concise, and clearly defined set of beliefs, values, and norms. The essential elements of this teaching are well known, so we may confine our discussion to those aspects which appear especially relevant to the problem of population control and family planning in contemporary society.

According to Catholic teaching, the vocation of marriage constitutes a particular or specific determination of the Christian's essential religious calling received at baptism. This basic Christian vocation is essentially an invitation to strive for perfection in the love of God and neighbor through union with Christ. Thus the couple's marriage vows, binding them to establish a procreative community of life and love, determine the distinctive elements in their general vocation as Christians, while the purposes of marriage as designed by the Creator define the special means through which they should express their love toward God and neighbor. It follows that Catholic family ideals can be fully understood only in terms of the entire Christian view of life, and any dimming of this view through secular influences is bound to undermine the conviction with which these ideals are held.

A further postulate of Catholic teaching is that the Creator designed the dual sexual nature of man with a double finality—parenthood and mutual fulfillment through a loving life-partnership—and marriage is the natural institution ordained to achieve this double finality. Christian thinkers have employed various expressions in stating this doctrine. Thus St. Augustine formulated his classic definition of the "goods" of marriage in the famous trilogy: conjugal fidelity, children, and indissoluble union. Centuries later, when explaining "the reasons because of which man and woman ought to be joined in marriage," the Catechism of the Council of Trent declared: "The first is precisely the companionship sought by the natural instinct of (each) different sex, and brought about by the hope of mutual aid, so that each may help the other to bear more easily the problems of life, and to support the weakness of old age. The second is the desire of having children." The present Code of Canon Law, employing a somewhat more precise legal approach, states that the primary purpose of marriage is the pro-creation and education of children, while its twofold secondary purpose is mutual service and the remedy of concupiscence (Canon 1013, No. 1).

Although this balanced, carefully formulated teaching of the Church should be clear enough, it seems that every generation produces its own peculiar misconceptions, misinterpretations, and one-sided emphases. The Church is so concerned with maintaining the correct definition of the nature and purposes of marriage because marriage is a sacrament. Since there are many possible types of association between men and women, it is necessary to make clear precisely what type of marital union Christ incorporated into his plan of salvation. The integral procreation-education process constitutes the primary—that is, the specifying—purpose of marriage because it is this process which constitutes the distinctive objective of that natural institution called marriage and which distinguishes it from all other possible types of association or partnership between men and women. Both the primary and secondary purposes of marriage are objective purposes; that is, they are ends or purposes inherent in the very structure of the institution. Technically speaking, however, the secondary purposes are called *secondary* because they are subordinate to the primary purpose in the sense that they are designed to assure its adequate fulfillment and receive their specifically marital qualities from their relationship to it.

Although this procreation-education process constitutes the primary purpose of marriage as an institution, it does not follow either as an ideal or as a safe moral norm that couples should attempt to have as many children as they are capable of procreating. All couples must bring the complete dedication of themselves to the purposes of marriage, but each couple will differ in the capacity to fulfill these purposes. For various reasons, some may have no children, or not so many as they desire; while others will have to judge prudently how many they can reasonably bear and raise to Christian maturity. This decision must be made within the broad moral framework of their general vocation as Christians and their special vocation as marital partners, but the responsibility of making it must rest with the individual couple concerned.

Thus while the Church insists on the centrality of the procreation-education process in defining the objective purposes of marriage, her teaching also stresses the importance of the personal ends; for considered from the viewpoint of the person, marriage is a means, not an end. Marriage by its nature as designed by the Creator has a double finality directing it toward the development and fulfillment of both the couple and their children. Fitting human procreation and education of children require a community of life between husband and wife based on mutual love, service, loyalty, and companionship. Hence mutual love, personal fulfillment, and the spiritual perfection of the partners are necessary objectives of marriage, but they receive their distinctive, specifying marital quality from their relationship to the primary purpose of this institution.

One further element of the Church's teaching merits some consideration here. The fundamental premise underlying the Catholic view of sexual morality is that there exists an essential relationship between marriage and the use of sex. To the extent that human sexual activity is the conscious, voluntary act of a responsible individual, it can achieve its full value and significance only if it is conjugal; that is, only if it is the expression and actualization of that community of life and love established by the human couple in marriage.

Two basic concerns have, consequently, dominated the thinking of moral theologians in formulating the Church's sexual norms. Briefly, they have aimed to protect human life in each and every form—thus their consistent condemnation of infanticide and abortion. Further, they have maintained a respect for "nature"; that is, they have recognized and accepted the need to respect the integrity of the inherent objective structure of the sexual act as designed by the Creator—thus their condemnation of any type of deliberate contraceptive interference with the normal physiological process freely initiated by the couple in the conjugal act.

The Church's stance regarding sexual morality is so well known that it merits no further comment here. Since recent controversies, however, concerning the morality of various new forms of physiological birth control reveal considerable confusion, it may be helpful to point out that wherever there is consideration of Catholic teaching in this area, one must distinguish between what the Church defines as moral doctrine and the precise reasoning by which the doctrine is demonstrated. Thus, although the Church teaches that contraceptive practices are immoral, theologians have not yet produced clear, convincing, universally accepted arguments based on moral principles derived from reason to prove that all possible types of such practices are always wrong.

This explains why theologians may not always agree in evaluating the moral licitness of new methods of intervening in the generative system. For example, they are currently discussing whether the "pill," assumed to inhibit ovulation, constitutes direct forbidden sterilization. The essential issue here is to determine how far man may go in regulating, controlling, or correcting the sterility-fertility cycle of the generative system.

A NOTE ON PLURALISM

The above observations regarding some relevant elements
of the Church's teaching on marriage are pertinent
because American Catholic couples must lead their lives
in a society characterized by moral pluralism. It should
be obvious that the American people no longer agree on
the meanings which they attach to marriage and family.
In this regard, we have what may be called a loosely
integrated culture. As anthropologist Linton has noted,
our "designs for living" are not clearly defined; our
cultural "blueprints for behavior" lack unity and con-
sistency. Or as sociologist Robin Williams describes it,
our society offers no relatively standardized prescriptions
as to what must be done, ought to be done, should be
done, may be done, and must not be done in matters
relating to sexual behavior, marriage, and family life.
In other words, individuals are presented with socially
acceptable alternatives in each of these categories, and
they may make their choices in terms of their own value
systems.

Such pluralism is not merely the result of rapid
social change or cultural lag. The origin of moral
pluralism lies in the realm of values. We can see this
clearly if we analyze any integrated social structure. Such
analysis reveals several elements of primary importance.
First, there is a basic set of beliefs relating to the origin,
nature, and destiny of man, the human agent. Further,
there are derivative sets of values and goals. These are
the social system's specific institutional objectives con-
stituting the culturally devised applications of the
above basic beliefs to various concrete social institutions
such as the economic, political, religious, familial, and

so on. Finally, we discover sets of institutionalized means. These include the culturally patterned and acceptable procedures, the clusters of social relationships established for the implementation of the approved institutional objectives.

For example, when we analyze any integrated family system, we find it involves a set of beliefs relating to the origin, nature and destiny of man; the specific marriage and family values derived from these beliefs; and definite patterns of conduct established so that these values can be attained by members of society. In other words, courtship practices, husband-wife and parent-child relationships are designed to actualize the marriage and family values of the group; and these values, in turn, are considered worth achieving because they are derived from the beliefs regarding human nature held by its members. Thus all definitions of human values ultimately stem from some conception of the nature of man. If people cherish different conceptions of human nature, they will logically define the nature and purposes of marriage differently and will consequently establish different patterns of conduct in relation to marriage. This indicates the profound significance of moral pluralism in the practical order.

SOCIAL FACTORS RELATING TO FAMILY REGULATIONS

Although procreative potential, as well as social organization and values, must be taken into consideration when studying problems of population control, it appears that the innate capacity to reproduce remains fairly similar among all the various segments of a given national group. Hence we must look to changes in our social institutions and systems of values if we are to grasp the crucial significance of family regulation for modern American couples. Let us review the more important of these changes briefly.

In the first place, American couples tend to marry relatively early; the average bride being twenty and her partner twenty-two. Although this decreasing age at marriage is probably related to our present economic prosperity, it is primarily the result of our contemporary dating and courtship patterns. Early cross-sex associations are so universally encouraged or tolerated that an increasing proportion of teenagers becomes emotionally or sexually involved and seeks to enter marriage. At the same time lack of adequate instruction and supervision results in a relatively high rate of premarital pregnancy; for in addition to the constantly mounting rates of illegitimacy and abortion, it is estimated that a considerable percentage of the younger brides are pregnant at marriage. Early marriage is significantly related to family regulation, inasmuch as it increases the couple's reproductive span. When couples marry young and start their families early in marriage—if not before—the wife's exposure to pregnancy period is correspondingly lengthened, while the probability that the missing virtue of prudent self-restraint will be acquired later is slight.

Second, infant and child mortality rates are so low that most children born will survive to maturity. Modern couples can count on raising the children whom they bear, and since the gains related to mortality have been achieved by better hospitalization, increased medical care, and more adequate diet, the economic cost of children has risen accordingly. Further, as the amount of formal education and training required for adequate participation in our highly technical, increasingly automated society steadily grows, parents must support their children during much longer periods than formerly.

Third, industrialization has radically affected the status and roles of children in the modern family. When production is for the market rather than for consumption, the locus of employment becomes the shop or factory, not the home, and the working unit becomes the individual laborer rather than the family. Under these circumstances, children cease to be productive. They become "mouths" rather than "hands," and since the wife can now enter the labor force only by working outside the home, the process of bearing and rearing children also prevents her from increasing the family income by holding a job. Thus children have a dual economic significance for the modern family; they prevent the wife from entering the labor force as so many other women are doing, and they are not only nonproductive but relatively costly in an urbanized setting.

Fourth, because of increased mobility and changes in the family system, young couples can now rely upon much less aid from their extended families. Relatives may help, but they are not obliged or expected to do so, and in many cases spatial distance and lack of funds render any form of assistance impossible. Thus such items as babysitting, sickness, hospitalization during childbirth, and so forth, present additional problems to the isolated modern family with several children.

Fifth, various factors in modern society have tended

to increase the significance of satisfactory marital relations in marriage, so that the regulation of family size through the practice of absolute continency apparently becomes more difficult than formerly. Among such factors are the changed attitudes of women in regard to the propriety of licit sexual pleasure, the increased need for conjugal companionship in the relatively isolated modern family, the lessening of shared activities in the domestic unit, the increase of sexual stimulation resulting from the relatively free association of men and women at work and play, and the persistent, calculated exploitation of the sexual drive in advertising, literature, dress, and entertainment. In connection with this latter point we might note that sex has come to preoccupy the modern American mind so excessively because of the serious, unresolved conflicts and tensions Americans personally experience as they continue to pay lip-service to traditional values and norms while tolerating or promoting contradictory standards in practice.

Finally, the general climate of opinion relating to the nature and purposes of marital relations has shifted radically. Implicit in this changed outlook is the assumption of two new postulates concerning human sexual activity. The first divorces the function of sex from its essential relationship to procreation, so that this purpose need no longer be respected in its use; the second takes sexual activity out of the realm of objective morality, so that the licitness of its various expressions is judged in terms of personal feeling rather than on the basis of an objective moral order designed by the Creator. The practical result of this shift is the widespread availability and acceptance of contraceptive birth control.

FACTORS RELEVANT TO FAMILY REGULATION AMONG CATHOLIC COUPLES

This is the society within which Catholic couples must live, love, and sanctify themselves in their marriage vocation. As members of society they must adjust to the social facts, but as Christians they cannot accept the dominant culture's solutions. Like most contemporary couples, they will probably marry young and start their families early. Perhaps more than others, they will tend to be spatially and socially mobile, moving out of the rapidly deteriorating industrialized urban centers where they have been traditionally concentrated, and using the educational ladder to climb out of the lower social-class status to which an immigrant background tended to confine their parents. Fully aware of the rising demands of our technically advanced society, they will be deeply in earnest about procuring good educational opportunities for their children, while at the same time they will strive to acquire some share in our contemporary affluence by accumulating the material symbols of success in terms of better housing and living standards for themselves.

These aspirations appear broadly legitimate, yet modern Catholic couples encounter serious difficulties in trying to achieve them. What are the major sources of their problems in this regard? In the first place, they may not make use of contraceptive birth control, which is the key solution which other couples employ in meeting problems related to family size. Second, many are neither adequately instructed nor prepared to face the practical implications of the profound changes resulting from recent developments in science and society. Both these sources merit further analysis. Let us begin with the first.

The contemporary social system is geared to the small family, so that housing, standards of living, recreational patterns, marital expectations, and so on, are patterned accordingly. Nevertheless, some accepted patterns of conduct run contrary to this tendency. Our increasingly early age at marriage, for example, is highly favorable to large families, as is the strong emphasis on infant and maternal health care. In the face of these contradictory practices, the small family ideal can be maintained only if there is consistent limitation of conception. This is presently achieved primarily through the widespread social acceptance and use of contraceptive devices, although induced abortions and sterilization apparently play no minor roles.

We can understand the practical implications of this situation for Catholic couples only if we recognize the key function which contraceptives fulfill in the social system. As contraceptive birth control gained acceptance and use, all the institutions and practices associated with the regulation of sex and parenthood became gradually adjusted and adapted to it. Thus the practice became institutionalized or geared into the whole social system as an integral part of its structures and values. Henceforth what might be termed *social equilibrium*, or the balance between accepted patterns of conduct and desired social goals, becomes established and maintained on the assumption that contraception will be widely used. If it is rejected, the whole system tends to be thrown off balance.

Let us look at how this practice functions in its present American context. For example, early age at marriage need not lead to large families, for couples may now limit their pregnancies. The present custom of "bunching" births early in marriage, usually before the wife is thirty, may be easily followed because family size can be planned. Since first pregnancies can be postponed, young wives may retain their jobs either in order to put their husbands through school or to increase the family income. In general, the maintenance of desired living standards, the "keeping up with the Jones" in dress, entertainment, housing, the education of children and so forth, becomes much easier if couples can limit family size when competing demands seem to require it.

On the other hand, the situation of Catholic couples in this context is fraught with difficulties. Their innate capacity to reproduce is similar to others. As members of society, they tend to accept prevailing cultural goals concerning standards of living, recreational patterns, marital expectations and so on. They find available the same type of housing and family income as other couples. At the same time, they also tend to follow present early dating and courtship customs, as well as the general emphasis on infant and maternal health care. Yet they may not accept their society's related values and means. The small-sized family as such is no Christian ideal; and even if it were to become so under changed circumstances, Catholic couples could not adopt contraceptive means to achieve it.

CONCLUSION

This all adds up to saying that if Catholic couples are to avoid serious difficulty in reconciling their innate reproductive capacity with their parental obligations under modern conditions, they must develop their own morally acceptable means for maintaining social balance or equilibrium. As we have suggested, however, many are ill-prepared to do so. Catholics as a whole have been slow to grasp the practical implications of pluralism or of recent social and scientific developments relating to parenthood. On the negative side, considerable time and effort have been expended on the refutation of aggressive birth control propaganda, but this has had the unfortunate effect of shifting attention away from basic issues and the development of a positive, integrated approach to the real problems which many Catholic couples must face.

Moreover, the negative attitude toward sex, so characteristic of some Christian teaching and early training, leaves couples poorly prepared to integrate sex, love, and self-control in marriage. When sex is regarded as a type of blind instinct rather than a normal human power, subject like all human faculties to rational control, it is not easily brought under the domination of love. Couples trained in a negative attitude toward sex find it difficult to regard the expression of love in marital relations as a valid expression of Christian love. Though they may not consider marital relations as evil, they tend to view them as a kind of natural activity never fully integrated in the total context of their love relationship as Christian spouses. Hence if abstinence is required, they find it difficult to regard the practice of self-control as an expression of Christian love.

Finally, the practice of periodic continence has generated such widespread controversies in this country, and inept attempts to use it have so frequently resulted in failure, that popular attitudes regarding it are characterized primarily by confusion and frustration. Couples still receive quite conflicting directives from various spiritual advisors concerning the licitness of the practice, while their sources of information regarding effective methods remain distressingly inadequate, if not highly misleading.

Given the distinctiveness of Catholic doctrines relating to marriage and the family, the moral pluralism characterizing contemporary society, and the various social changes and developments making some type of family regulation imperative for the majority of fertile young couples, we may conclude that the continued observance of Christian marriage ideals appears likely only if Catholic couples acquire a more adequate understanding and appreciation of the Church's positive doctrine concerning the vocation of marriage, together with the firm conviction that this doctrine remains currently relevant. Since effective use, moreover, of presently available methods of practicing periodic continence requires considerable knowledge of each wife's cycle-patterns, together with training and experience in mutual adjustment and self-control, young adults have the right and obligation to acquire adequate understanding of the moral and medical aspects of licit family planning. Fertile young couples should not wait until they have reached what they feel to be their procreative "limit" before looking about for some licit, easily manageable means of family regulation—but there are none such currently available.

GEORGE B. WILSON

Christian Conjugal Morality
and Contraception

My immediate concern as a teacher and student is Sacramental Theology and since I am not immediately involved
with moral theology, much less with the specific problem
of population control, the presence of this chapter calls
for some explanation and perhaps even for a defense. To
satisfy this need I would simply point to the title of this
book: we are concerned here with "*Christian* social ethics."
As Christians we believe that no question fundamental to
man's moral life can be solved, or even adequately
formulated, in abstraction from the Biblical revelation
about man's relation to God, and since our immediate
problem is so intimately linked to the institution of
marriage, the presence of someone interested in the full
sacramentality of marriage as presented in the Bible
would seem not a luxury but a necessity for the study of
such a question in a Christian context. It will be my task
here to suggest some considerations and questions with
which we must reckon if we are to understand the ultimate

foundations for any answers which may be reached on the morality of various approaches to population control. Perhaps we can illustrate the general area of my reflections by quoting for you some rather Madison-Avenuish titles which occurred to me when I undertook this chapter: "Surely There's More to Christian Marriage Than Natural Law?"; "Is That All the Church Can Say about Marriage?"; "Christian Marriage Is *Also* a Sacrament"; "The Bible's Teaching on Marriage Doesn't Sound Like That"; or only half in jest, "Can't Theologians Talk to Christian Couples about Anything but the Pill?"

As is immediately evident from the general direction of these titles, our concern here will be to investigate the content of revelation concerning the nature of marriage; then with that specific area in mind I would like to throw some light on the requisites of a Christian ethics in general; and finally, we will perhaps be able to deepen our understanding of the precise contradiction involved in contraception when it is practised by Christian couples and, more importantly, suggest some ideas about the role of Christian married couples. I will be the first to admit that these considerations will seem far removed from the global problem of population control and that they will probably raise more questions than they solve. But I will be satisfied if we come to realize that these *are* the fundamental realities with which we must come to grips if Christian revelation is to have anything to say to our exploding world.

I. THE BIBLICAL REVELATION CONCERNING MARRIAGE

Obviously it will be impossible here to go into any great detail in presenting the divine conception of marriage as

presented in Scripture. We shall have to content ourselves
with the broad lines accepted by Scripture scholars.

The first point to be made would be that, as Fr. Grelot
has observed, the Scriptural message about marriage is
not primarily an ethical, much less a sociological, one;
it is directly *religious* in its intention. That is to say that the
empirical phenomena of the Israelite marital mores, the
Israelite code of law in sexual matters, the polygamy of
the Patriarchs, the gradual purification of conjugal
ethics—all of these things are really secondary and can
be paralleled in other contemporary cultures. What is
unique to the Israelites is that God reveals to them a new
religious meaning for man's sexual love. He reveals to them
a direct, new relationship between man's affective and
generative powers and his service of the one God who
is Yahweh. It is true that sex is sacred for all the ancient
peoples, but it gets its specific meaning from the *kind* of
religion which sacralizes it and the *way* the peculiar reality
of sexual love is inserted into the divine order of things.
Thus, it does not surprise us if a religion whose gods were
male and female, who could mate with one another in
countless combinations, would inspire a different cult of
sexual fertility than does the unique almighty Yahweh who
transcends all sexual difference and creates out of perfectly
selfless love. At any rate, the Israelite in his Scriptures sees
sex and marriage as intimately related to the service of
the one, true, living God, and this, not simply because of
a moral code imposed upon the reality of marriage more
or less arbitrarily and from without, but because of the
intrinsic nature of the reality itself. Down through the
growth in biblical revelation, we find a unique mutual
interdependence between the revelation of the ideal of

human marriage and the clearer understanding of our real relation to God. While the true ideal of human marriage is being purified despite slow progress in the empirical sociological order, the Prophets are simultaneously revealing that this ideal is itself a figure or analog to teach us of the union which God is establishing with His People. The people are the bride, the spouse, the beloved of Yahweh, and the perfection of His love for them serves in its turn to teach them how selfless and creative human marital love is meant to become. Remaining within the created order, sexual love in marriage contains within itself nonetheless the power to disclose to man God's stance of love toward mankind, if only man can see it fully for what it is; of course, communication of this fact and the power to grasp it which we call faith are God's pure gift.

And God goes even further in bringing into close conjunction these two areas so deeply rooted in man's being—his response to the mystery of his own human sexual attraction and marital fulfillment—God takes human marital love and makes it the means of revealing to man the attitude of intimate love which He, Yahweh, has freely assumed toward mankind. This causality is mutual: it is precisely because God uses this reality as a symbol for His own stance of love that we learn, not only what is the ideal or goal toward which the finite marital love is tending, but also the capacity which it possesses to reveal to us, however dimly, a reality which transcends all human experience, God's own self-communication to man.

This growing revelation reaches its peak in the Incarnation, when the Son of God assumes human nature, institutes His Church as His own Body and also as His

Bride. In the fifth chapter of Ephesians, St. Paul plumbs the mystery of human marriage to its last depth when he realizes that marriage is only an imperfect re-presentation of the real nuptial mystery to which it has been pointing all along: the union of Christ and His Church. It is this union which is perfect marriage, a union so intimate that the Church and Christ really form one principle of operation, one organism. All human marriage is but an image of this union, approaching its perfection of selfless creative love only more or less imperfectly. And note that I say *all* marriage, not just Christian marriage. This is the burden of the new insight: that marriage has been pointing to this ideal all along, even though it was hidden from the beginning (as it is still hidden from countless couples today, who are nonetheless by their love symbolizing this perfect union in their own imperfect ways). Beyond the mere unconscious representation involved in every marriage, Christian marriage, insofar as it is between baptised persons living out their baptismal commitment to Christ, effectively re-actualizes this life-giving union of Christ and His People in the here-and-now of everyday life.

Even as sketchy as such an outline is, it should alert us to the fact that if this is the way Christian revelation views *all* marriage, no adequate Christian ethic can be built on the basis of natural law alone even when our understanding of that law is aided by all the scientific knowledge which man can bring to bear from the fields of sociology, demography, psychology, and so forth, and even when the Church herself is declaring that law to us. Christian revelation *does* have more to say to man about marriage than simply to declare the criteria by which he

can judge between sin and non-sin in the use of his affective, generative faculties. This becomes clearer when we
situate this revelation about God's plan for marriage by
relation to other areas of Christian theology, which is
our second consideration.

II. THE TENSION OF THE CHRISTIAN WORLD-VIEW

When we range over the various elements of Christian
anthropology, we are met constantly by a tension which
is uniquely Christian. We know from the whole Christian
understanding of the redemptive love of Christ that God
intends for man a destiny which far surpasses all his
natural powers—the communication of the divine life
itself to man. We also know from another area of revelation that even man's natural powers have been infected
by his sinfulness; the whole order of nature as intended
by God has been disrupted and must be healed. From
these reflections the Church has come to realize that Christ
by His self-communication which we call grace effects a
double task: He heals the wounds in man's natural powers
and thus we speak of the *healing* function of grace. But
He also enables this healed human nature to achieve an
end which is beyond its unaided (even healthy) natural
powers and so we say that grace also *elevates* man to the
supernatural level. The Christian tension involves *living*
this polarity in such a way that we do not destroy or negate
either pole. If we then turn our attention to the theological formulation of another mystery, namely God's
presence in the world, we must say in the light of the
Incarnation that God has chosen out of love to make Himself *immanent* to the created world of man; but He also

remains obviously *transcendent* to that world, perfectly and inalienably one with His creation and yet utterly "other," and surpassing it by a difference infinitely greater than any humanly conceived likeness. Once again, when we express this same tension in terms of the Christian's attitude to the world about him, we say that it must be at once *Incarnational* (for God *is* present to His creation, the whole of creation is redeemed and healed in Christ) and yet *eschatological* (this world and its highest values, even when healed by Christ, remain finite and natural and are to be ultimately surpassed by the "new creation," by a world in which these values are transcended).

When we bring all these different questions together, we can express this tension synthetically in terms of the *natural* and *supernatural,* or concretely in terms of grace and nature. The Christian may not live in a purely natural world; he must receive supernatural help *even* to achieve the perfection of his natural capacities and even then that achievement is not enough for him because God has summoned him to transcend the perfection of the natural order.

Of course all of this is ultimately rooted in the mystery of Christ Himself as at once perfectly human and perfectly divine, the mystery of selfless, creative, and redemptive love perfected on the Cross and continuing in a sacramental, but all the more real, way in the life of His Church.

When we translate this once again to the level of the Christian's general attitude to this world and its values, we can describe the basic tension in all Christian virtue in this way: the Christian has the task of tending toward the transcendent, eschatological, supernatural values in such a way that he gives full assent and true esteem to the natural values which are being transcended; or to take the opposite side of the same coin, he must strive to realize a fully healed natural order while always realizing the primacy of the supernatural and being open to the divine invitation to effect that eschatological good here and now. The Christian may be invited to forego his own personal enjoyment of these values "for the sake of the kingdom of heaven" but he does so as a Christian only if he sets the highest value on what he offers to God, and on the other hand, no virtuous adherence to true human values is truly Christian unless it includes at least the willingness to offer these goods at the divine invitation.

Perhaps these apparently very remote considerations will take on greater meaning if we relate them to the particular area of conjugal love as viewed in the light of our first analysis, with a particular application to the immediate question concerning the contradiction of contraception for Christian couples.

III. A CHRISTIAN VIEW OF MARRIAGE AND CONTRACEPTION

Returning now to the idea that all marriage is an imperfect realization (in Platonic terms a participation, in Scriptural terms a figure) of the perfect marriage which is the union of Christ and His Church, we have but to recall that in the final achievement of that union, human sexual differentiation and sexual love will play no role: "They will neither marry nor be given in marriage"—"There will be neither male nor female." Relating this to our general analysis of the Christian tension, we see that the truly Christian view of sexual love will always include two elements: the

full endorsement of human love as the highest natural
fulfillment of man's personality and natural powers, but
accompanied by the acknowledgment that even this
supreme natural fulfillment is tending under God's gift
and invitation toward a love which transcends sexual
expression, without ever making that expression thereby
a second-class value.

This does not mean, as some have suggested, that
the expression of love in marriage has a natural tendency
to develop from intercourse to a stage in which genital
union is no longer "needed," or is "transcended" in
that sense; much less does it mean that married couples
ought to aim to arrive at that highly dubious goal. There
is in such thought, I suspect, a latent Manicheanism.
Christian revelation says nothing about such a goal or
tendency toward it *within* the earthly life of the married
couple. It does tell us, however: 1) that when the kingdom
of God is finally consummated there will be no sexual
union, and 2) that even within this era, God may call some
individuals to witness to that absolute kingship of His by
loving all men and indeed humanly, without sexual
union. For the Christian married couple this carries the
implication that they may not make of sexual union,
sacramental as it may be, an *absolute* which in effect
excludes the possibility that God may through circumstances be calling them to forego this expression; no
matter how positively and even religiously they may be
oriented toward the sexual expression of love, they must
be at least *open* to the possibility of such a call or else they
have in fact made of sex an absolute, an idol.

And it must be stressed that the actuation of this
tension is necessary for Christian virtue wherever it is to

be realized. *All* Christians are called to testify to the world, by word and action, that this is the kind of value they place on the sexual expression of human love. (The same could be verified in the case of man's use of the wealth of this world and the value of human free self-determination.) Perhaps unwittingly we have created the impression that only the consecrated celibate is to testify to the eschatological transcendence of sex, while the Christian married couple would testify to the goodness of this lofty natural good as healed by Christ; then somehow the two "half-witnesses" put together would equal the Church's revelation to the world concerning this sphere of reality. But half-virtues are non-virtues. Such a schizophrenic vision of Christian virtue is impossible. If the celibate may not look down on human sexual love and still be a Christian (and he may not: Christian sacrifice is the offering of a *good* to God), neither may the married couple make such an absolute of human sexual fulfillment that their life is in this respect to all intents and purposes a rejection of the primacy of God's kingship and His right to ask temporary or even lasting abstinence from enjoyment of this good. The truth is that wherever virtue is to be Christian it must express both natural goodness and supernatural transcendence, the incarnational healing of all that is truly human and its eschatological fulfillment; in short, the human and divine at work in the world since God's redeeming love became incarnate in Christ.

We arrive at last at the question of contraception. In the light of our general analysis of the tension involved in the Christian world-view and the religious significance of marriage and the sexual expression of love, we are perhaps in a position to put forward a *theo-logical*—as opposed to a biological—definition of contraception. We are, after all, concerned with the deepest foundations of *Christian* moral judgment. Theologically I would define contraception as the use of the human faculty for sexual expression of human personal love in marriage in such a way as to make this expression effectively an absolute value, closed to the intervention of God's invitation to sacrifice, whether that sacrifice take the form of the responsibility for children or the abstaining from sexual intercourse. I leave it to those more competent than I in the science of moral theology to decide *where* this contraceptive distortion is actually verified in reality, whether it is possible that it be verified in a single act or only in a more pervasive personal attitude and decision; whether the use of these means or those necessarily attests its presence or not, and so forth. I believe it is also a matter for the philosophers and ethicians to see if this contraceptive assessment of sexual fulfillment contradicts even man's nature as known by the light of reason alone. (I think it does.) What must be clear is that for a Christian ethic such an evaluation is a contradiction of the rest of the *Christian's* professed view of life, and that this contradiction is indeed the most fundamental reason for its sinfulness. To enter a union which is a human continuation and extension of the union between Christ and the Church, while denying to that union its supernatural tendency to transcend the merely human in openness to Christian sacrifice, is to embrace an impossibility.

Population Growth and
Its Implications:
A Bibliography

Adam, A., *Der Primat der Liebe; eine Untersuchung uber die Einordnung der Sexualmoral in das Sittengesetz.* Bonn; 1939.

Adelman, Irma, "An Econometric Analysis of Population Growth," *American Economic Review*, June, 1963, pp. 314–339.

American Academy of Political and Social Science. "A Crowding Hemisphere: Population Change in the Americas." *Annals of the American Academy of Political and Social Science.* March, 1958.

American Assembly, *The Population Dilemma.* Englewood Cliffs, N. J.; 1963.

Approaches to Problems of High Fertility in Agrarian Societies, Milbank Memorial Fund, 1952.

Aptekar, Herbert, *Anjea: Infanticide, Abortion, and Contraception in Savage Society.* New York; 1931.

Augustine, *St. Augustine: Treatises on Marriage and Other Subjects*, translated by C. T. Wilcox, *et. al.*, New York. Fathers of the Church, 1955.

Avalos, Beatrice, *New Men for New Times*. New York; 1962.

Ayres, E., and Scarlott, C., *Energy Sources, The Wealth of the World*. New York; 1952.

Baade, Fritz, *The Race to the Year 2000*; Our Future: A Paradise or the Suicide of Mankind. Garden City, N.Y.; 1962.

Back, K. W., Hill, Reuben, and Stycos, J. M., "The Dynamics of Family Planning," *Marriage and Family Living*, August, 1956.

Bailey, Derrick Sherwin, *Common Sense about Sexual Ethics*. London; 1962.

———, *Man-Woman Relationship in Christian Thought*. London; 1959.

———, Bailey, D. S., "Marriage and the Family: Some Theological Considerations," in *The Human Sum*, ed. by C. H. Rolph. New York; 1957.

———, *The Mystery of Love and Marriage*. New York; 1952.

———, *Sexual Ethics: A Christian View*. New York; 1963.

———, *Sexual Relations in Christian Thought*. New York; 1959.

Bainton, Roland H., *What Christianity Says about Sex, Love and Marriage*. New York; 1959.

Barclay, George W., *Colonial Development and Population in Taiwan*. Princeton; 1954.

———, *Techniques of Population Analysis*. New York, 1955.

Barnett, H. J., and Morse, C., *Scarcity and Growth*. Baltimore; 1963.

Barnett, Robert W., "Population Growth and Economic Development," *Department of State Bulletin*, 12/7/62.

Barooch, Ramesh Chandra, *The Demographic Aspects of*

Family Planning. Shillong; 1962.

Barrett, Donald N. *The Problem of Population.* South Bend; 1964.

Barth, Karl, *Die Kirchliche Dogmatik,* III. Zurich; 1951. Esp. Part 4.

Bates, Marston, *Expanding Population in a Shrinking World.* New York; 1963.

———, *The Prevalence of People.* New York; 1955.

Batzill, Hartmann, O.S.B., *Decisiones Sanctae Sedis de Usu et Abusu Matrimonii.* Turin; 1944.

Baum, Gregory, O.S.B., *Progress and Perspectives.* New York; 1964.

Baxter, William J., *Wages Are Going Lower.* New York; 1951.

Belshaw, Horace, *Population Growth and Levels of Consumption with Special Reference to Countries in Asia.* London; 1956.

Benedict, M. R., "Population and Food: Precarious Balance," *Foreign Policy Bulletin,* 8/1/59.

Bennett, Merill, *The World's Food.* New York; 1954.

Bertocci, P. A., "Extra-Marital Sex and the Pill," *Christian Century,* 2/26/64.

Bertram, G. C. L., *Population Trends and the World's Biological Resources.* London; 1949.

Billington, James H., *Mikhailovsky and Russian Population.* Oxford; 1958.

Blake, Judith, *Family Structure in Jamaica: The Social Context of Reproduction.* Glencoe, Ill., 1961.

Bogue, D. J., *Population Growth in Standard Metropolitan Areas: 1900–1950.* U.S. Housing and Home Finance Agency. Washington; 1953.

———, *The Population of the United States.* Glencoe, Ill.; 1959.

———, (ed.) *Applications of Demography: The Population Situation in the U.S. in 1975*. Oxford, Ohio. Scripps Foundation of Research in Population Problems, 1957.

Bouscaren, Timothy L., and A. C. Ellis. *Canon Law: A Text and Commentary*. Milwaukee; 1957.

Bouscaren, T. L., *Canon Law Digest*. (vol. III), Milwaukee; 1954.

———, "Discussion of Canon 88," *Periodica*, 33, 1944.

———, *Ethics of Ectopic Operations*. Chicago; 1933.

Borrie, Wilfrid David, *The World's Population: Perspective and Prospect*. Toronto; 1961.

Bowen, Ian, *Population*. London; 1954.

Bowman, Henry Adalbert, *A Christian Interpretation of Marriage*. Philadelphia; 1959.

———, *Marriage for Moderns*. New York; 1960.

Brody, S., *Bioenergetics and Growth*. New York; 1945.

Brown, Harrison, *The Challenge of Man's Future*. New York; 1954.

———, Bonner, J., and Wier, J., *The Next Hundred Years*. New York; 1957.

Brown, Lester R., *Man, Land & Food*. Foreign Agricultural Economic Report 11, U.S. Department of Agriculture, 1963.

Buckley, Joseph, *Christian Design for Sex Principles and Attitudes for Parents and Teachers*. Chicago; 1952.

Burch, Guy Irving, *Population, Road to Peace or War*. Washington; 1945.

Burch, Thomas K., "Patterns of Induced Abortion and Their Socio-Moral Implications in Postwar Japan," *Social Compass*, vol. 3, no. 4, 1955.

Cabot, Richard, *Christianity and Sex*. New York; 1928.

Caffarel, Henri, *Love and Grace in Marriage*. Notre Dame;

1960.

Calderone, M., "An Inventory of Contraceptive Methods Adapted to Public Health Practice," *American Journal of Public Health,* 52 (10).

California Institute of Technology, *Resources of the World, A Speculative Projection.* Pasadena, 1956.

Capper, W. M., *Toward Christian Marriage.* Chicago; 1958.

Carney, Francis, *The Purposes of Christian Marriage.* Washington; 1950.

Carnegie Institute of Technology, *Selected Readings in Problems of Population.* Pittsburgh, 1941.

Carpenter, R., *Relative Population Densities and Immigration Policy of the United States.* Buffalo, 1925.

Carr, Aiden, "The Morality of Situation Ethics," *Proceedings of the Catholic Theological Society of America,* XII (1957).

Carr, N. (pseud.), *Birth Control in Marriage.* Chicago: Medical Bureaus of Information on Birth Control, 1931.

Carr-Saunders, A. M., *The Population Problem.* Oxford; 1922.

——, *World Population: Past Growth and Present Trends.* Oxford; 1936.

Casey, T. J., "Catholics and Family Planning," *American Catholic Social Review,* June, 1959.

Cervantes, Lucius F., S.J., *And God Made Man and Woman.* Chicago; 1959.

Chandrasekhar, S., *Population and Planned Parenthood in India.* London; 1955.

Chanson, Paul, *L'accord charnel.* Paris, 1950.

——, *L'Étreinte reservée: témoignage des époux.* Paris, 1951.

Chen, Kuan I., *World Population and Living Standards.* New York; 1960.

Chisolm, Brock, "The Population Explosion," in *World Union Goodwill*, vol. 2, October, 1962.

Clapham, John Harold, *The Historian Looks Forward*. London; 1942.

Coale, Ansley J., Hoover, Edgar M., *Population Growth and Economic Development in Low-Income Countries*. Princeton; 1958.

Coggle, B. J., *Christian Social Ethics*. London; 1956.

Cohausz, Otto, *The Pope and the Christian Marriage*. New York; 1933.

Colby, Charles Carlyle, *Geographic Aspects of International Relations*. Chicago; 1938.

Cole, William Graham, *Sex in Christianity and Psychoanalysis*. New York; 1955.

Conference on *Psychological Mechanisms Concerned with Conception*. A Symposium. Population Council and Planned Parenthood Federation of America, 1958.

Conference on Research in Family Planning. New York; 1960.

Conference on *World Population and Birth Control*. New York Academy of Sciences, 1952.

Connell, F., "Unusual Statement about Contraception," *American Ecclesiastical Review*, July, 1963.

———, "The Contraceptive Pill," *American Ecclesiastical Review*, 137 (1957).

———, *Father Connell Answers Moral Questions*. Washington; 1959.

———, "The Morality of Ovulation Rebound," *American Ecclesiastical Review*, September, 1960.

Connery, John R., S.J., "Notes on Moral Theology," *Theological Studies*, 15, 1954.

———, "Notes on Moral Theology," *Theological Studies*, 17, 1956.

———, "Notes on Moral Theology," *Theological Studies*,

19, 1958.

———, "Notes on Moral Theology," *Theological Studies*, 20, 1959.

Conquest, P., *Soviet Deportation of Nationalities*. New York; 1960.

"Control of Human Fertility," *Impact* (UNESCO publication)2.

"Control of World Population Growth," *Washington Population Research Project*. Washington; 1963.

Conway, James, S.J., *The Fundamental Principles of Christian Ethics*. Chicago.

Conway, William, "The Recent Papal Allocution: The Ends of Marriage," *Irish Theological Quarterly*, 19, 1952.

Cook, Robert Carter, "Baby Boom Decade, 1946–1955," *Population Bulletin*, May, 1957.

———, *Human Fertility: The Modern Dilemma*. New York; 1951.

———, *Population and Food Supply*. United Nations, 1962.

———, "Recession in Births?", *Population Bulletin*, October, 1958.

Coontz, Sidney H., *Population Theories and Economic Interpretation*. London; 1957.

Coulet, P. A. E., *Les Problèmes de la fécondité humaine*. Paris; 1953.

Cottrell, William F., *Energy and Society: The Relation Between Energy, Social Change, and Economic Development*. New York; 1955.

Cox, Peter R., *Demography*. Cambridge; 1959.

Creusen, Joseph, S.J., "L'enseignement du magistère ordinaire," *Nouvelle Revue Théologique*, 559, 1932. (Onanism in marriage.)

Cronin, John, *Social Principles and Economic Life*. Milwaukee; 1959.

Current Population Survey Reinterview Program: Some Notes and Discussion. Washington; 1963.

Dahlberg, Gunnar, *Mathematical Methods for Population Genetics*. New York; 1948.

Darwin, Sir Charles Galton, "Forecasting the Future," *Engineering and Science*, April, 1956.

———, *The Next Million Years*. New York; 1952.

———, *The Problems of World Population*. Cambridge, 1958.

Daven, Thomas Herbert, *Disease and Population Pressure in the Tropics*. Ibadan, Nigeria; 1958.

Davis, Henry, *Birth Control Ethics*. London; 1927.

———, *Moral and Pastoral Theology*, (Vol. II.), London; 1948.

Davis, Kingsley, "The Amazing Decline of Mortality in Underdeveloped Countries," *American Economic Review*, May, 1956.

———, "A Crowding Hemisphere: Population Changes in the Americas," *Annals of the American Academy of Political and Social Science*, March, 1958.

———, "Future Population Trends and Their Significance," *Transactions of the Eighteenth North American Wildlife Conference*, 1953.

———, "Population," *Scientific American*, September, 1963.

———, *The Population of India and Pakistan*. Princeton; 1951.

Dawnson, F. James, *Aggression and Population*. London; 1941.

de Castro, J., *The Geography of Hunger*. Boston; 1952.

Deevey, E. S., "Human Population," *Science*, September, 1960.

de Lestapis, Stanislas, S. J., "Crise de surpopulation mondiale?", *Revue del l'action populaire*, April, 1959.

———, *L'enciclique casti connubii*. Paris; 1955.

———, *Family Planning and Modern Problems*. New York; 1961.

———, "Les mouvements familiaux dans le monde," *Cahiers de pastorale familiale*, 1957, no. 4.

———, *Les vraies valeurs de la vie conjugale*. Paris; 1953.

Demographic and Economic Change in Developed Countries. (A Conference of the Universities – National Bureau of Economic Research.) Princeton; 1960.

Denziger-Rahner, *Enchiridion Symbolorum*. Edition 31a. Barcelon, Rome, Fribourg; 1957.

Deploige, Simon, *The Conflict Between Ethics and Sociology*. St. Louis; 1938.

de Smet, Alois, *De Sponsalibus et Matrimonio*. Brugis; 1927.

Desmond, Annabelle, *How Many People Have Ever Lived on Earth?* Washington: Smithsonian Institute, Annual Report, 1962.

Dewhurst, J. F., *America's Needs and Resources: A New Survey*. New York; 1955.

Dickenson, R. L., "Conception Control," *Journal of the American Medical Association*, 12/18/43.

Dickinson, J., and Smith, G., "A New and Practical Oral Contraceptive Agent: Norethindrone with Mestranol," *Canadian Medical Association Journal*, 89 (6), 1963.

Does Over-Population Mean Poverty? The Facts about Population Growth and Economic Development. Washington Center for Determining Economic Growth, 1962.

Dorn, H. F., "Pitfalls in Population Forecasts and Projections," *Journal of the American Statistical Association*, September, 1950.

Dougherty, Dudley Tarlton, *The Water Problem, a*

Solution. Philadelphia; 1957.

Dowring, F., "Opportunity to Multiply: Demographic Aspects of Modern Colonialism," *Journal of Economic History*, December, 1961.

Drogat, Noel, *The Challenge of Hunger.* Westminster, Md.; 1962.

Dublin, L., and Lotka, A. J., *Length of Life.* New York; 1949.

Duhamel, Joseph, S. J., "The Catholic Church and Birth Control," *In the Eyes of Others.* New York; 1962.

Duncan, Otis Dudley and Spengler, Joseph J., *Population Theory and Policy.* Glencoe, Ill.; 1956.

Durand, John, *The Labor Force in the United States, 1890–1960.* New York; 1948.

Dyer, Isadore, *Ethical and Religious Directives for Catholic Hospitals.* St. Louis; 1956.

Eizenga, Weitze, *Demographic Factors and Savings.* Amsterdam; 1961.

Eldridge, Hope T., *The Materials of Demography.* New York; 1959.

———, *Population Policies.* Washington: International Union for the Scientific Study of Population, 1954.

Errington, P. L., "Of Man and the Lower Animals," *Yale Review*, March, 1962.

Ewell, Raymond, "Role of Research in Economic Growth," *Chemistry and Engineering News*, 33:29, 1955.

Fagley, Richard N., *The Population Explosion and Christian Responsibility.* New York; 1960.

Family in Contemporary Society. (Report for the Bishops of the Lambeth Conference, 1958.) London; 1958.

Farraher, Joseph, S. J., "Notes on Moral Theology," *Theological Studies*, 16, December, 1955.

———, "Notes on Moral Theology," *Theological Studies*,

21, December, 1960.

———, "Notes on Moral Theology," *Theological Studies*, 22, December, 1961.

Fawcett, Charles Burgay, *The Numbers and Distribution of Mankind*. Smithsonian Institution, Annual Report, 1948.

Fertility Abstracts. Monthly. Published by Family Centre Ltd., London.

Findings of Studies on the Relationships between Population Trends and Economic and Social Factors. Lake Success; 1950.

Finney, Patrick, and O'Brien, C. M., *Moral Problems in Hospital Practice*. St. Louis; 1956.

Fisher, Joseph L., and Edward Boorstein, *The Adequacy of Resources for Economic Growth in the United States*. Washington: U.S. Government Printing Office, 1959.

Fletcher, Joseph, *Morals and Medicine*. Princeton; 1954.

Flugel, J. C., *Men and Their Motives*. New York; 1947.

———, *Population and Peace*. London: C. A. Watts, 1947.

Foerster, Friedrich Wilhelm, *Marriage and the Sex Problem*. New York; 1936.

Food and Agriculture – World Conditions and Prospects. F.A.O., 1949.

Ford, John C., S. J., and Kelly, Gerald, S. J., *Contemporary Moral Theology*, Vol. II – "Marriage Questtions," Westminster, Md.; 1961.

Forsyth, William Douglass, *The Myth of Open Spaces*. Melbourne and London; 1942.

Francis, Roy G. (ed.), *The Population Ahead*. Minneapolis; 1958.

Frankel, S. H., *The Economic Impact on Underdeveloped Countries*. Cambridge, 1953.

Freedman, Ronald, Pascal K. Whelpton, and Arthur A. Campbell, *Family Planning, Sterility, and Population Growth.* New York; 1959.

Frumkin, Gregorz, *Population Changes in Europe Since 1939.* New York; 1951.

Fuchs, Joseph, S. J., *De Castitate et Ordine Sexuali.* Rome; 1960.

——, *Die Sexualethik des Heiligen Thomas von Aquin.* Cologne; 1949.

Galbraith, John Kenneth, *The Affluent Society.* Boston; 1958.

Gallagher, Conan, "Sexual Pleasure: Its Proper Setting in Christian Marriage," *American Ecclesiastical Review,* May, 1962.

Gandhi, Mohandos Karamchand, *Birth Control.* Bombay: 1962.

Gardner, Richard N., "Politics of Population: A Blueprint for International Cooperation," (Address of May 4, 1963.) *Department of State Bulletin,* June 10, 1963.

——, *Population Growth, a World Problem: Statement of U.S. Policy.* Washington; 1963.

Geisert, Harold L., *The Control of World Population Growth.* Washington; 1963.

——, *Population Growth and International Migration.* Washington; 1962.

——, *World Population Pressures.* Washington; 1958.

Georg, I. E., *The Truth About Rhythm.* New York; 1962.

Gernier, Joseph, *Du Principe de Population.* Paris; 1957.

Gerrard, Thomas John, *Marriage and Parenthood, the Catholic Ideal.* New York; 1951.

——, "Fertility Control in the Light of Some Recent Catholic Statements," *Eugenics Quarterly,* March,

1956 and June, 1956.

———, and Burch, Thomas K., "Physiologic Control of Fertility: Processes and Morality," *American Ecclesiastical Review*, April, 1958.

———, *Population, Resources, and the Future*. New York; 1961.

Gibbs, Jack P. (ed.), *Urban Research*. Princeton; 1961.

Ginsburg, Norman E., *Atlas of Economic Development*. Chicago; 1961.

Ginzberg, Eli, *et al.*, *Occupational Choice*. New York; 1951.

Glass, David Victor, *Introduction to Malthus*. London; 1953.

———, *The Struggle for Population*. Oxford; 1936.

———, *The Universal Teaching of Social Sciences; Demography*, Paris; 1957.

Glick, Paul C., *American Families*. New York; 1957.

Goldstein, Sidney, *The Meaning of Marriage and Foundations of the Family*. New York; 1942.

Gottman, Jean, *Megalopolis: The Urbanized Northeastern Seaboard of the United States*. New York; 1961.

Grabill, Wilson H., Kiser, Clyde V., and Whelpton, Pascal K., *The Fertility of American Women*. New York; 1958.

Greek Orthodox Handbook, 1958. New York; 1958.

Greenberg, D. S., "Birth Control: Swedish Government Has Ambitious Program to Offer Help to Underdeveloped Nations," *Science*, 9/28/62.

———, "The Population Explosion: Bishop's Proposal to Study Conflicts with Some Popular Conception of Church," *Science*, 10/30/62.

Greep, Roy O. (ed.), *Human Fertility and Population Problems*. Mass.; 1963.

Gregg, Alan, "A Medical Aspect of the Population

Problem," *Science*, CXXI:682, (1955).

Grelot, Pierre, *Man and Wife in Scripture*. New York; 1964.

Guttmacher, Alan F., *The Complete Book of Birth Control*. New York; 1961.

Hajnal, J., "Age at Marriage and Proportions Marrying," *Population Studies*, November, 1953.

———, "The Marriage Boom," *Population Index*, April, 1953.

Halbwachs, Maurice, *Population and Society: Introduction to Social Morphology*. Glencoe, Ill.; 1960.

Hanson, E. P., *New Worlds Emerging*. New York; 1951.

Haring, Bernard, *The Law of Christ*. Westminster, Md.; 1962.

Harte, Thomas J., *Papal Principles*. Milwaukee; 1956.

Hartman, C. G., *World Population Problems and Birth Control*. New York; 1952.

Hatt, Paul K. (ed.), *World Population and Future Resources*. New York; 1952.

Hauser, Philip M. (ed.), *Population and World Politics*. Glencoe, Ill.; 1958.

———, *The Population Explosion*. New Brunswick, N. J.; 1960.

———, *Population Perspectives*. New Brunswick, N. J.; 1960.

——— and Duncan, Otis Dudley (eds.), *The Study of Population*. Chicago; 1959.

Hawkins, Denis J. B., *Man and Morals*. New York; 1961.

Healy, Edwin, S.J., *Marriage Guidance*. Chicago; 1958.

Heinen, G., *Orale Kontrazeption*. Medizinische Welt 40:2089.

Helmig, Dennis M., "Special Report: The Population Challenge," *Report*, June, 1964.

Henle, Mary, "A Psychological Concept of Freedom:

Footnotes to Spinoza," *Social Research*, Fall, 1960.

Henshaw, Paul S., *Adaptive Human Fertility*. New York; 1955.

———, "Increasing Child Population Poses New Problem for UNICEF," *Review*, April, 1959.

———, "Physiologic Control of Fertility," *Science*, 5/29/53.

Hertzler, J. O., *The Crisis in World Population*. Lincoln; 1956.

Hewetson, John, "Birth Control, Sexual Morality, and Abortion," *Twentieth Century*, Winter, 1963.

Higbee, Edward. *The Squeeze: Cities Without Space*. New York; 1960.

Hildebrand, Dietrich von, "Die Idee der sittlichen Handlung," *Jahrbücher für Philosophie und Phenomenologische Forschung*. Halle, 1916.

———, *In Defense of Purity*. London; 1931.

———, *Marriage*. New York; 1942.

———, "Marriage and Overpopulation," *Thought*, Spring, 1961.

———, *Sittlichkeit und ethische Verkenntnis*. Halle, 1921.

Hill, Reuben, Stycos, J. J., and Back, Kurt W., *The Family and Population Control: A Puerto Rican Experiment in Social Change*. Chapel Hill; 1959.

Hinman, Helen R., and William I. Battin, Jr., *Population Pressure, War and Poverty*. Newark, N.J.; 1945.

Himes, Norman E., *A Medical History of Contraception*. Baltimore: Williams & Wilkins, 1936. (Paper, New York; 1964.)

Holt, J. G. H., *Marriage and Periodic Abstinence*. London; 1960.

Hook, Sidney, "Philosophy and Human Conduct," *Kenyon Review*, Fall, 1960.

Huber, Paulette. *The Teachings of Pius XII on Marriage and the Family.* Washington; 1950.

Hudeszek, M. M., "De Tempore animationis foetus humani secondum embryoloiam hodiernam," *Angelicum*, April–June, 1952.

Huerth, Francis, S. J., "Inquisitio critica in mora itatem 'Amplexus Reservati'," *Periodica* 41, 1952.

——, *De re matrimoniali.* Rome; 1955.

——, "De Sterilitate Physiologica," *Nouvelle revue théologique*, 58, 1931.

Huxley, Aldous, *Brave New World.* New York; 1960.

Huxley, Julian, *The Human Crisis.* Seattle; 1963.

——, *New Bottles for New Wine.* New York; 1957.

Huyck, Earl, and James Brackett, "The Objectives of Government Policies on Fertility Control in Eastern Europe," *Population Studies*, November, 1962.

Isaac, Julius, *The Economics of Migration.* New York; 1947.

Ishii, Ryoichi, *Population Pressure and Economic Life in Japan.* London; 1937.

Jacobs, Jane, *The Death and Life of Great American Cities.* New York; 1961.

Jacobson, Paul H., *American Marriage and Divorce.* New York; 1959.

Jaffe, Abram J., *People, Jobs, and Economic Development: A Case History of Puerto Rico, Supplemented by Recent Mexican Experience.* Glencoe, Ill.; 1959.

Jarrett, Henry (ed.), *Perspectives on Conservation: Essays on America's Natural Resources.* Baltimore; 1958.

Jenkins, Daniel T. (ed.), *The Doctor's Profession.* London; 1949.

Johann, Robert O., S. J., *The Meaning of Love.* Westminster, Md.; 1955.

Jones, M. D., and Howard, W., "The Arithmetic of the

Rhythm Method of Contraception," *Current Medical Digest*, May, 1964.

Joyce, G. H., *Christian Marriage: An Historical and Doctrinal Study*. New York; 1933.

Kelly, George A., *Birth Control and Catholics*. New York; 1963.

————, *Overpopulation: A Catholic View*. New York; 1960.

Kelly, Gerald, S. J., "The Common Good and the Socio-Economic Order," *Proceedings of the Catholic Theological Society of America*, VII. 1952

————, "Confusion: Contraception and the Pill," *Theology Digest*, XII, Summer, 1964.

————, *Medico-Moral Problems*. St. Louis; 1958.

Kerns, Joseph. *The Theology of Marriage: the Historical Development of Christian Attitudes Towards Sex and Marriage* New York: Sheed & Ward, 1964.

Kinsey, Alfred, *Sexual Behavior in the Human Male*. Philadelphia; 1948.

Kiser, Clyde V. (ed.), *Family Planning*. Princeton; 1962.

Krempel, A., *La Continence periodique: Traite élémentaire á l'usage des epoux et de leurs conseillers: Knaus, Ogino, Smulders*. Mulhouse; 1954.

Krempel, Bernardin, *Die Zweckfrage der Ehe in neuer Beleuchtung*. Zurich and Koln; 1941.

Kuznets, Simon Smith, *Population Redistribution and Economic Growth: United States, 1870–1950*. Philadelphia: American Philosophical Society, 1957.

Lambeth Conference, 1867–1930. London; 1948.

————, *1930*. New York; 1930.

————, *1958*. New York; 1958.

Landis, Paul Henry, *Population Problems, a Cultural Interpretation*. New York; 1948.

Latz, Leo J., *The Rhythm of Sterility and Fertility in Woman*. Chicago, 1932.

Lavell, Carr, *Population Growth and Development of South America*. Washington; 1959.

Leclerq, Jacques, *Du droit naturel à la sociologie*. Paris; 1960.

————, *Marriage and the Family*. New York; 1949.

Lepp, Ignace, *The Psychology of Loving*. Westminster, Md.; 1963.

Lewis, Arthur W., *The Theory of Economic Growth*. London; 1955.

Li, Ching-chun, *Population Genetics*. Chicago; 1955.

Liebenstein, Harvey, *Economic Backwardness and Economic Growth*. New York; 1957.

————, *A Theory of Economic-Demographic Development*. Princeton; 1954.

Lindner, Dominikus, "Der Usus Matrimonii," *Sune Sittliche Bewertung in Katolischen Moraltheologie alter und neuer Zeit*. Munich; 1927.

Lohkamp, Nicholas, *The Morality of Hysterectomy Operations*. Washington; 1956.

Lonergan, Bernard, S.J., "Finality, Love, Marriage," *Theological Studies*, 4, 1943.

Lorimer, Frank, *et al.*, *Culture and Human Fertility*. Paris; 1954.

————, and Frederick Osborn, *Dynamics of Population*. 1934.

————, *et al.*, "An Inquiry Concerning Some Ethical Principles Relating to Human Reproduction," *Social Compass* IV, Nos. 5–6.

————, *Population Trends in the Soviet Union*. League of Nations, 1946.

————, *The Problems of Changing Population*. National Resources Committee, 1938.

Lowenthal, David, and Lambras Comitas, "Emigration

ohn T., *Contraception*. Cambridge, Mass.; 1965.

incent J. (ed.), *Christian Marriage: Some Contem-*
y Problems. Jamaica, N.Y.; 1961.

adnar, *Problems of Capital Formation in Under-*
ped Countries. Oxford; 1953.

. A., *Natural Birth Control Without Contraceptives,*
ding to Nature's Law, In Harmony with Catholic
ity. Champaign, Ill.; 1938.

l, Thomas, S.J., *Morals in Medicine*. West-
er, Md.; 1960.

ue, J., *World Population Growth and Living*
ards.. New York; 1960.

Population Research, Princeton University;
Population Association of America, Inc.,
ation Index. Published quarterly.

rnard, *Trends in Birth Rates in the United States*
1870. Baltimore; 1958.

Marc, *Union in Marital Love*. New York; 1958.

ie chrétienne et problèmes de la sexualité. Paris;

S. H., *Resources and the American Dream*. New
; 1953.

A. F. K., and Katherine Organski, *Population*
World Power. New York; 1962.

airfield, *The Limits of the Earth*. Boston; 1953.

d.), *Our Crowded Planet: Essays on the Pressures*
ulation. Garden City, N. Y.; 1962.

ur *Plundered Planet*. Boston; 1948.

,000 *More Every 24 Hours*. New York; 1951.

Frederick (ed.), *Population: An International*
ama. New York; 1958.

reface to Eugenics. New York; 1951.

his Crowded World. Public Affairs Pamphlet, No.

and Depopulation," *Population Review*, July, 1962.

Lynch, John J., S.J., "Fertility Control and the Moral
Law," *Linacre Quarterly*, August, 1953.

————, "Moral Aspects of Fertility Control," *Proceed-*
ings of the Thirteenth Annual Convention of the Catholic
Theological Society of America, 1958.

————, "Progestational Steroids: Some Moral Problems,"
Linacre Quarterly, August, 1958.

Mace, David R., *Hebrew Marriage*. New York; 1953.

Madigan, John M., S.J., *Intersexuality and Its Moral Aspects*,
Rome; 1956.

Mair, G. F. (ed.), *Studies in Population*. Princeton; 1949.

Mallory, Robert, and Theodore Irwin, *Modern Birth Control*.
New York; 1961.

Malthus, Thomas, *On Population*. New York; 1960.

————, Julian Huxley and Frederick Osborn, *Three Essays*
on Population. New York; 1960.

Marshall, John, M.D., *The Infertile Period*. Westminster,
Md.; 1963.

Mason, Edward S., *Energy Requirements and Economic*
Growth. Washington; 1955.

Matsumoto, S., Nogami, Y., and Ohkuri, S., "Statistical
Studies in Menstruation," *Gunma Journal of Medical*
Science, ii:4.

Mauroux, Jean, *The Meaning of Man*. New York; 1961.

Maury, Marian (ed.), *Birth Rate and Birth Right*. New York;
1963.

Mayer, Andre, *et al.*, *Food and People: Seven Essays*. London;
1950.

Mayer, K., "Fertility Changes and Population Changes in
the United States," *Social Research*, Autumn, 1959.

McAuley, Claire, *Whom God Has Not Joined*. New York;
1961.

McAuliffe, Michael F., *Catholic Moral Teaching on the Nature of Conjugal Love*. Washington; 1954.

McClintoch, Charles Graham, *World Population Pressures*. Technological Military Planning Operation, General Electric Co.: Santa Barbara, Calif., 1958.

McCormack, Arthur (ed.), *Christian Responsibility and World Poverty*. Westminster, Md.; 1963.

————, "Paul VI and Overpopulation," *Studies*, Fall, 1963.

————, *People, Space, Food*. New York; 1960.

————, *World Poverty and the Christian*. New York; 1963.

McDougall, Frank L., *Food and Population*. New York; 1952.

McKelvey, V. E., "Resources, Population Growth, and Level of Living," *Science*, 4/3/59.

Mears, E., "A New Type of Oral Contraceptive," (Volidan) *British Medical Journal*, 89:6, 1963.

Meier, Richard L., *Modern Science and the Human Fertility Problem*. New York; 1959.

————, *Science and Economic Development*. New York; 1956.

Merkelbach, B. H., *Questiones de embryologia et de sterilisatione*. Liege; 1937.

Mertens, C., "Problèmes de Population: croître ou vieillir," *La Revue Nouvelle*, 4/15/59.

Messenger, E. C., *Two in One Flesh*, vol. III. Westminster, Md.; 1948.

Messner, J., *Social Ethics*. St. Louis; 1952.

Meyerson, Martin, Barbara Terrett and William L. C. Wheaton, *Housing, People, and Cities*. New York; 1962.

Mezerik, A. G., *Food and Population: International Program, National Action*. New York; 1963.

Milbank Memorial Fun
    Europe, the USSR a
    1960.

Mitrany, David, *Food and*

Monsma, John Clover, *F*
    City, N.Y.; 1963.

Morrison, W. A., "At
    towards Family Plan
    Milbank Memorial Fu

Muller, Lyer-Franz, *Th*
    New York; 1930.

Mulvaney, Bernard, *Co*
    Between the Catholi
    Its Birth Rate. Urba

Murphy, A. C., "Abort
    A Medico-Moral Vi

Murphy, John, *The Rhyt*
    York; 1955.

Myrdal, Gunnar, *Popu*
    Gloucester, Mass.;

National Bureau of Eco
    Series #II, "Demo
    in Developed Cou

Nevett, Albert, *The*
    Leicester, S. Walke

"A New Anti-Fertility F

"New Birth Control
    Letter, 4/11/64.

Niebuhr, Reinhold, *The*
    Nature (Vol. I). (G

Notestein, F. W., "Tl
    the Year 2000,"
    Association, Septem

Noon;
Nuger
    A
Nursk
    de
O'Brie
    A
    M
O'Don
    m
O'Don
    St
Office
    an
    Po
Okun,
    sin
Oraiso
————,
    19
Ordway
    Yo
Organsl
    and
Osborn,
————,
    of F
————,
————,
Osborn,
    Dile
————,
————,

306. Public Affairs Committee, Inc. New York, December, 1960.

Oser, Jacob, *Must Men Starve? The Malthusian Controversy.* London; 1956.

Palazzini, Pietro, *et al.*, "Una Donna Domanda Come Negarsi alla Violenza?" *Studi Cattolici*, November-December, 1961.

Palmieri, Dominicus, *Tractatus de Matrimonio Christiano.* Rome; 1880.

Parkes, A. S., "Change and Control in Human Populations," *Eugenics Review*, April, 1963.

Parrish, John Bishop, *Some Aspects of the Relationship Between Real Wages and the Supply of Labor.* Urbana, Ill.; 1938.

Pearl, R., *The Biology of Population Growth.* New York; 1925.

———, *The Natural History of Population.* New York; 1939.

———, *Population.* New York; 1961.

Peterson, Arthur, *The Politics of Population.* Garden City, N.Y.; 1964.

Phelps, Harold Augustus, *Population in Its Human Aspects.* New York; 1958.

Piddington, Robert Alfred, *The Limits of Mankind.* Bristol; 1956.

Pieper, Josef, "Protestant Attitudes on Contraception," *Proceedings of the Catholic Theological Society of America*, XV, 1960.

Pincus, Gregory, *et al.*, "Effectiveness of an Oral Contraceptive," *Science*, 7/10/59.

———, (ed.), *The Hormones* (Vol. II). New York; 1950.

Piper, Otto A., *The Biblical View of Sex and Marriage.* New York; 1960.

———, *The Christian Interpretation of Sex.* New York; 1941.

Pius XI, Pope, "Casti Connubii," encyclical letter. *Acta Apostolicae Sedis*, 22 (1930), 539–592.

Pius XII, Pope, "Address to the Hematologists," September 12, 1958. *Acta Apostolicae Sedis*, 50 (1958), 732–740.

————, "Address to the Italian Society of Urologists." *Acta Apostolicae Sedis*, 45 (1953), 674ff.

————, "Address to the Midwives." *Acta Apostolicae Sedis*, 43 (1951), 835– 854.

————, "Address to the Tenth National Convention of the Italian Society of Plastic Surgery." *Acta Apostolicae Sedis*, 50 (1958), 952–961.

————, Radio Message of Pentecost, June 1, 1941. *Acta Apostolicae Sedis*, 33 (1941), 216–227.

Planque, Daniel, *The Theology of Sex in Marriage.* Notre Dame, Ind.; 1962.

Political and Economic Planning (PEP). *World Population and Resources.* London; 1955.

Popenoe, Paul, "Family or Companionate," *Journal of Social Hygiene*, vol. IX, no. 3.

"Population Control," *Law and Contemporary Problems*, Summer, 1960. Durham, N. C.

"Population Explosion: Bishiops' Proposal For Study Conflicts With Some Popular Conceptions of The Church," *Science* 138 (1962) 960–961.

"Population Problem Reviewed," *Linacre Quarterly*, February, 1964.

Population Reference Bureau, Inc. *Population Bulletin.* Monthly.

Population Studies. London. Three issues annually.

Proceedings of the 5th International Conference on Planned Parenthood: Tokyo, 1955. London; 1956.

Quay, Paul M., S.J., "Contraception and Conjugal

Love," *Theological Studies*, 22, 1961.

——, *Contraception and Marital Love*. Washington; 1962.

Quisenberry, K. S., *Crop Production Potentials in Relation to Freedom from Want*. Waltham, Mass.; 1948.

Raab, Earl, and Selznick, G. J., *Major Social Problems*. New York; 1964.

Rade, P., *Die Stellung des Christentums zum Geschlechtsleben*. Tübingen, J. C. B. Mohr, 1910.

Rainwater, Lee, *And the Poor Get Children*. Chicago; 1960.

Ramirez, D., and McCann, S. M., "A Highly Sensitive Test for LH Releasing Activity," *Endocrinology*, 73:2, 1963.

Ramsey, Paul, *Nine Modern Moralists*. Englewood Cliffs, N. J.; 1962.

Rehwinkel, A. M., *Planned Parenthood and Birth Control in the Light of Christian Ethics*. St Louis; 1959.

"Rhythm Method Doomed," *Science News Letter*, 2/15/64.

Rice-Wray, E., *et al.*, "Oral Progestins in Fertility Controls, A Comparative Study," *Journal of Fertility and Sterility*, 14:4.

Riker, Audrey and Charles, *Understanding Marriage*. Glen Rock, N. J.; 1963.

Robbins, John, *Too Many Asians*. Garden City, N.Y.; 1959.

Roberti, Francesco Cardinal, *Dictionary of Moral Theology*. Westminster, Md.; 1962.

Roberts, George W., *The Population of Jamaica*. Cambridge; 1957.

Rock, John, M.D., *The Time Has Come*. New York; 1963.

Rockefeller Brothers Fund. *Foreign Economic Policy for the Twentieth Century*. New York; 1958.

Roe, Ann, *The Psychology of Occupations*. New York; 1956.

Rosen, J., and M. Eastman, *The Road to Abundance*. New York; 1953.

Ryan, John, *Family Limitation*. London; 1960.

Ryan, John, *Medical Aspects of Marriage*. London; 1951.

Sanger, Margaret, *The Case for Birth Control*. New York; 1917.

Sauvy, Alfred, *Fertility and Survival: Population Problems from Malthus to Mao Tse-Tung*. New York; 1961.

———, *Théorie générale de la population*. Paris; 1952–54.

Sax, Karl, "The Population Explosion," *Headline Series* 120. New York: Foreign Policy Association, 1956.

———, *Standing Room Only*. Boston; 1957.

Schahl, Claude, *La Doctrine des fins du mariage dans la théologie scholastique*. Paris; 1948.

Schillebeeck, E., *Marriage*. New York; 1965.

Schimm, Melvin, *Population Control, The Imminent World Crisis*. New York; 1961.

Schmiedler, Edgar, *Christian Marriage*. Washington; 1939.

———, *An Introductory Study of the Family*. New York, 1947.

———, *Marriage and the Family*. New York; 1946.

Schultz, Theodore W. (ed.), *Food for the World*. Chicago; 1945.

Schwartz, D., *et al.*, "Clinical Experience with a New Oral Contraceptive," *Journal of Fertility and Sterility*, 14:3, 1963.

Selected Readings in Problems of Population, Pittsburgh; 1941.

Senior, Clarence, *Land Reform and Democracy*. Gainesville, Florida; 1958.

Seward, Georgene, *Sex and the Social Order*. New York; 1946.

Sheps, M., "Changes in Birth Rate as a Function of Contraceptive Effectiveness: Some Applications of a Stochastic Model," *American Journal of Public Health*, 53:7, 1963.

Sheridan, Edward F., S. J., *The Morality of the Pleasure Motive in the Use of Marriage.* Rome; 1947.

Shoulson, A. B., *Marriage and Family Life.* New York; 1959.

Siegel. T., "Conception Control by Long-acting Progrestogens: A Preliminary Report."

Smith, John, "The Permanent Truth in the Idea of Natural Religion," *Harvard Theological Review,* January, 1961.

Smith, Kenneth, *The Malthusian Controversy.* London; 1951.

Smith, Thomas, *Fundamentals of Population Study.* Chicago; 1950.

——, *Population Analysis.* New York; 1948.

Snoeck, A., "Hesperidin and the Moral Law," *Theology Digest,* Spring, 1954.

Spengler, Joseph J. (ed.), *Natural Resources and Economic Growth.* Washington; 1961.

Spengler, J. J., and Duncan, Otis Dudley (eds.), *Demographic Analysis: Selected Readings.* Glencoe, Ill.: 1956.

——, *Population Theory and Policy.* Glencoe, Ill.; 1956.

Staley, Eugene, *The Future of Underdeveloped Countries: Political Implications of Economic Development.* New York; 1954.

Stamp, L. D., *Land for Tomorrow.* Bloomington; 1952.

Stamp, Lawrence, *Our Developing World.* London; 1960.

Starling, E. H., *Principles of Physiology.* Philadelphia; 1956.

Stephens, R. W., *Population Pressures in Africa South of the Sahara.* Washington; 1959.

Steuart, Sir James, *On Population,* from *An Inquiry into the Principles of Political Economy.* In *Source Readings in Economic Thought.* New York; 1954.

St. John-Stevas, Norman, *Birth Control and Public Policy.* Santa Barbara, Calif.; 1960.

Stockwell, E. G., "Relationship Between Population Growth and Economic Development," *American Sociological Review*, April, 1962.

Stone, A., and Himes, N. E., *Planned Parenthood*. New York; 1951.

Strauss, C. B., "Population Growth and Economic Development," *South African Journal of Economics*, June, 1963.

Stuart, Alexander, *Overpopulation: Twentieth Century Nemesis*. New York; 1958.

Stycos, J. Mayone, *Family and Fertility in Puerto Rico*. New York; 1955.

——, "Some Directions for Research on Fertility Control," *Milbank Memorial Fund Quarterly,* April, 1958.

Suenens, Leon-Joseph, Cardinal, *Love and Control*. Westminster, Md.; 1961.

Sulloway, Alvah W., *Birth Control and Catholic Doctrine*. Boston; 1959.

Sutherland, Halliday Gibson, *Birth Control*. New York; 1922.

Suy, Erik, "Legality, Morality and Natural Law," *World Justice* March, 1963.

Taeuber, Conrad and Irene, *The Changing Population of the United States*. New York; 1957.

Taeuber, Irene, *The Population of Japan*. Princeton; 1958.

Taft, Donald, and Robbins, Richard, *International Migrations*. New York; 1955.

Tarver, James D., *A Component Method of Estimating and Projecting State and Subdivisional Population*. Stillwater, Okla.; 1959.

Taylor, Rosalie, "The Premarital Consultation," *Marriage Guidance*, February, 1956.

Terman, L. M., *Psychological Factors in Marital Happiness.* New York; 1938.

Tertullian, *Treatises on Marriage and Remarriage.* (Ancient Christian Writers #15) Westminster, Md.; 1951.

Thomas, John L., S. J., *Catholic Viewpoint on Marriage and the Family.* Garden City, N.Y.; 1958.

——, *Marriage and Rhythm.* Westminster, Md.; 1957.

——, *Religion and the American People.* Westminster, Md.; 1963.

Thompson, J. Walter, *Population and Its Distribution.* New York; 1961.

Thompson, Warren S., *Population: A Study in Malthusianism.* New York; 1945.

——, *Population and Peace in the Pacific.* Chicago; 1946.

——, *Population and Progress in the Far East.* Chicago; 1959.

——, *Population Problems.* New York; 1953.

Thomson, C., *A Christian Approach to Family Planning.* Madras; 1963.

Timlin, Bartholomew, *Conditional Matrimonial Consent.* Washington; 1934.

Tokuhata, G. K., *Behavioral Factors Affecting Fertility Expectations: Introduction to Behavioral Demography.* Ann Arbor; 1956.

Toner, Jules, "Focus for Contemporary Ethics," *Thought*, Spring, 1964.

Torrey, E. F., "Artificial Insemination: Problem in Medical Ethics," *Medical Digest*, June, 1964.

Tracy, S.J., *et al.*, *A Report on World Population Migrations.* Washington; 1956.

Transactions of the Third Meeting of the Fertility Club of

Northern Countries, Stockholm, 1962. Some articles published in *International Journal of Fertility*, 7:3, 4.

Trevett, Reginald, *The Church and Sex*. New York; 1960.

————, *The Tree of Life: Sexuality and the Growth of Personality*. New York; 1963.

United Nations, Department of Economic and Social Affairs. *Demographic Yearbook*. Published annually.

————, *The Determinants and Consequences of Population Trends*. (Population Studies, 17) New York, 1953.

————, *The Future Growth of World Population*. New York, 1958.

————, *Handbook of Population Census Methods*. (Studies in Methods, Series F. no. 5.) New York, 1954.

————, *Handbook of Vital Statistics Methods*. (Studies in Methods, Series F. no. 7.) New York, 1955.

————, *Report on the World Social Situation*; With Special Reference to the Problems of Balanced Social and Economic Development. New York, 1961.

Urner, J. B., *Fertility Reduction and Economic Growth in Underdeveloped Countries*. Chicago; 1958.

"L'URSS et sa population," *Population*, (numero special), June, 1958.

Vann, Gerald, *The Heart of Man*. Garden City, N.Y.; 1950.

————, *Morals and Man*. New York; 1960.

Velde, T. H. van de., *Sexual Tensions in Marriage*. New York; 1948.

Venning, G.R. "World Population", *Lancet*, 1:637, 1962.

Villard, Henry, *Economic Development*. New York; 1959.

Vogt, William, *People: Challenge to Survival*. New York; 1960.

von Hildebrand, Dietrich, "Marriage and Overpopulation," *Thought*, Spring, 1961.

Wellin, P., and Clark, A., "A Study of Orgasm as a Condition of Women's Enjoyment of Coitus in the Middle Years of Marriage," *Human Biology*, 35:2, 1963.

Ward, Barbara, *The Rich Nations and the Poor Nations*. New York; 1962.

Warner, Hugh C., "Theological Issues of Contraception," *Theology*, 57, 1954.

Waytinsky, Wladimer, and Emma, *World Population and Production: Trends and Outlook*. New York; 1953.

Weatherhead, Leslie, *The Mastery of Sex Through Psychology and Religion*. New York; 1932.

Weintraub, Robert, "The Birth Rate and Economic Development," *Econometrica*, October, 1962.

Werth, Alvin, *Papal Pronouncements on Marriage and the Family*. Milwaukee; 1955.

Westoff, Charles F., *et al.*, *Family Growth in Metropolitan Areas*. Princeton; 1961.

———, *et al.*, "Preferences in Size of Family and Eventual Fertility Twenty Years After," *American Journal of Sociology*, March, 1957.

Westow, Theodore L., *The Variety of Catholic Attitudes*. Herder & Herder, 1963.

Whelpton, Pascal K., *Cohort Fertility*. Princeton; 1954.

White, C. L., "World Population, World Hunger, and World Resources," *Vital Speeches of the Day*, 5/15/59.

Whitworth, Geoffrey, *The Great Refusal, A Challenge to Depopulation*. London; 1942.

Wilkin, Vincent, S. J., *The Image of God in Sex*. New York; 1955.

Williams, Glanville, *The Sanctity of Life and the Criminal Law*. New York; 1957.

Williamson, Harold F., and Buttrick, John A. (eds.), *Economic Development: Principles and Patterns*. New

York; 1954.

Winslow, C. E. A., *War and Epidemics*. Princeton; 1952.

Wolfle, Dael, *America's Resources of Specialized Talent*. New York; 1954.

———, "Manpower Statistics," *Science*, 1/13/56.

World Population Conference, Rome, 1954. *Proceedings*. New York; 1956.

Wright, H., *Sex Fulfillment in Married Women*. London; 1948.

Wrong, Dennis, *Population and Society*. New York; 1961.

Wylie, William P., *Human Nature and Christian Marriage*. New York; 1958.

Yaukey, David, *Fertility Differences in a Modernizing Country: A Survey of Lebanese Couples*. Princeton; 1961.

Yearbook of Obstetrics and Gynecology. Chicago.

Zimmerman, Anthony F., "Birth Control in Japan," *World Justice*, September, 1963.

———, *Catholic Viewpoint on Overpopulation*. Garden City, N. Y.; 1961.

———, "Moral conjugale et progestogènes," *Ephemerides Theologiae, Louvanienses*, October–December, 1963.

———, "Morality and the Problem of Overpopulation," *Proceedings of the Catholic Theological Society of America*, 1959.

———, *Overpopulation: A Study of Papal Teachings on the Problem with Special Reference to Japan*. Washington; 1957.

———, "Some Reasons Why the Church Opposes Contraception," *American Ecclesiastical Review*, April, 1964.

Zimmerman, Carle C., and Lucius Cervantes, *Marriage and the Family*. Chicago; 1956.

The Contributors

LESTER R. BROWN was born in 1934 on a farm near Bridgeton, New Jersey. He worked his way through college under a combination of scholarships and part-time farming. In 1956 he was selected as a U.S. International Farm Youth Exchange delegate to India where he spent the fall and winter of 1956, living in the villages. He received his Masters Degree from the University of Maryland in 1959 and then entered the Department of Agriculture, serving as a country specialist for the southeast Asian countries. In 1961 his division was transferred to the Economic Research Service. After graduate studies at Harvard University, Mr. Brown was Regional Economist for the Far East and South Asia Branch, Assistant to the Deputy Director of the Foreign Regional Analysis Division, Assistant to the Administrator of Economic Research Service, and Staff Economist in the Office of the Secretary. His two books, *Man, Land and Food*, and *Increasing World Food Output*, are basic reference work on world food needs and on agricultural development problems in developing countries. Among his many honors, he was awarded in 1965 the Agriculture Department's Superior Service Award for "extraordinary professional competence, as exemplified by recent research contributions to the clearer understanding of future world food problems." In November, 1966, Mr. Brown became administrator of the International Agricultural Development Service.

FRANCIS X. QUINN, S.J., was born in 1932, entered the Society of Jesus in 1950 and was ordained in 1963. He received his A.B. and M.A. degrees from Fordham University, an S.T.B. from Woodstock College and an M.S.I.R. from Loyola University of Chicago. In 1959 he was awarded the Teacher of the Year citation from Freedom Foundation. He is a member of the Federal Mediation and Conciliation Service, a member of the American Arbitration Association, and at present is a Manpower Fellow at Temple University, Philadelphia. He has edited two earlier symposia, *The Ethical Aftermath of Automation* (1962) and *Ethics, Advertising, and Responsibility* (1963). His articles on social problems have appeared in such journals as *Social Order, Social Justice Review, Social Digest,* and *The Theologian.*

DR. ALICE M. RIVLIN was born in Philadelphia, Pennsylvania, and grew up in Bloomington, Indiana. A graduate of Bryn Mawr College, she received her doctorate in economics from Radcliffe in 1958. She is now Deputy Assistant Secretary for Program Analysis in the Department of Health, Education and Welfare.

She has also been a research director at the Brookings Institution; a Teaching Fellow and Tutor in Economics at Harvard University; a consultant to the House Committee on Education and Labor; a member of the Panel of Consultants to the Secretary of the Treasury; and a member of the staff of the Advisory Commission on Intergovernmental Relations. Dr. Rivlin is also the author of *The Role of the Federal Government in Financing Higher Education*, as well as other books, articles, and reports on various economic subjects.

DR. IRENE B. TAEUBER is Senior Research Demographer of the Office of Population Research at Princeton University. She received her liberal arts degree from the University of Missouri, her Master of Arts from Northwestern University and her doctorate (Ph.D.) from the University of Minnesota. Dr. Taeuber has been with the Office of Population Research at Princeton University since its establishment in 1936 and has undertaken major research in the western Pacific, including Japan, China, and the Chinese-related cultures of the Pacific littoral. She has also undertaken major research in the United States. Her recent major publications include: *The Population of Japan* (1958), *The Changing Population of the United States* (with C. Taeuber), and *Population Trends in the United States, 1900–1960* (1965). In 1966 she received from the University of Minnesota its Regents Award for Distinguished Achievement, and also was Chairman of the Population Symposia, Pacific Science Congress, in Tokyo. During the fall of 1966, in the Far East, she did research on demographic modernization in the Chinese and Chinese-related populations of the perimeter of Mainland China.

JOHN L. THOMAS, S.J., is Research Associate at the Cambridge Center for Social Studies. He holds degrees in English and French literature, philosophy, theology, and sociology, has studied Catholic social movements in postwar Europe, held a Guggenheim Fellowship (1953–1954), and served as President of the American Catholic Sociological Society (1959–1960). His various publications include *The American Catholic Family, Marriage and Rhythm, The Catholic Viewpoint on Marriage and the Family, Religion and the American People, Looking toward Marriage*, as well as numerous monographs and papers. He is presently engaged in studying the historical development of Christian views relating to human sexuality.

GEORGE, B. WILSON, S.J., was born in Philadelphia, Pennsylvania, and entered the Society of Jesus in 1946. During his preparatory studies in the Society he followed the course of philosophical studies and classical languages at St. Louis University. He received his Master of Arts in the Classical Languages there in 1953 and held the position of Instructor of Philosophy at the University of Scranton from 1953 to 1956. Father Wilson then continued his preparatory studies in the Society of Jesus by studying theology at the University of Innsbruck, Austria, and later at Woodstock College in Maryland. From 1961 to 1963 he pursued further studies in theology at the Gregorian University in Rome and received his doctorate there in 1963. He then joined the faculty at Woodstock College as Professor of Dogmatic Theology, specializing in the theology of the Church and Marriage.